≈ # Unsettling Relations

## The University as a Site of Feminist Struggles

*by*
*Himani Bannerji,*
*Linda Carty,*
*Kari Dehli,*
*Susan Heald,*
*Kate McKenna*

SOUTH END PRESS
BOSTON, MA

produced by the Women's Press collective
copy editing and proofreading by P.K. Murphy
cover design by Denise Maxwell
cover photograph of women's rally supplied by Canadian Women's Movement Archives/Archives canadiennes du mouvement des femmes

This book originated in Canada by Women's Press, 517 College Street, Suite 233, Toronto, Ontario, Canada M6G 4A2. Women's Press gratefully acknowledges financial support from the Canada Council and the Ontario Arts Council.

U.S. LIBRARY OF CONGRESS CATALOGING-IN-PUBLICATION DATA

Unsettling relations : the university as a site of feminist struggle / Himani Bannerji ... [et al.].
    p.  cm.
    Includes bibliographical references.
    ISBN 0-89608-453-1 : $30 (cloth)—ISBN 0-89608-452-3 : $12 (pbk.)
    1. Women—Education (Higher)—Social aspects. 2. Women—Education (Higher)—Political aspects. 3. Critical pedagogy. 4. Feminist theory—Study and teaching (Higher) 5. Women college teachers.
    I. Bannerji, Himani.
LC1567.U58   1992                                    92-25424
                                                     CIP


    8 7 6 5 4 3 2 1      92 93 94 95 96 97 98 99

SOUTH END PRESS, 116 Saint Botolph Street, Boston, MA 02115

# Contents

. . . . . . . . . . . . . . . . . . . . . . . . . . .

## ≈ Introduction

**· · · · · · · · · · · · · · · · · · · · · · · · · · · · · · · · ·**

The five authors of this book have at different times had connections to the same graduate school at a time when feminist theory and sociological practices were — and still are — being questioned. While some of us met for the first time when we began this writing project, others have become familiar with each other and each other's work over a period of years, meeting in different contexts inside and outside university classrooms. Undertaking this project, we discovered that we had common questions and issues, although we now work in different places and do our political and academic work quite differently. We share a political project vis-a-vis universities as sites of struggle, while recognising that they are also sites for the reproduction of power and privilege. It is at this point, however, that the commonalities end. We have come to recognize and respect our differences in experience and approach, realizing their significance through working together and discussing each other's work.

One of our aims in writing this book is to contribute to debates among feminists within and outside the university and to the politics of building coalitions among women. We remain loyal to different communities outside academia, communities where we feel a sense of belonging and political commitment. This too is part of the struggle: to include analyses and experiences that rarely get voiced in academia and to do so in ways that do not simply exploit women's experiences and stories as "data."

This introduction comes out of discussions taped as we worked on this book. Re-reading the transcripts and notes of our talks, we have picked out themes that connect our work and our politics. We think of ourselves as feminist activists and analysts, and although we have worked on very different topics and used a range of methodologies and theoretical perspectives, we centre analyses of class and race relations in our feminisms. Implicitly or explicitly we draw on the work of Marx and of marxist feminists. In this book, we write from different locations as participants in the social relations and practices of power in the university. We ask how these social relations and practices are actually put together; to begin to answer and analyze that question we talk about how we have lived them. From this shared methodological starting point, we try to show how social relations and practices of domination and oppression — and at times of struggle and empowerment — are being produced and reproduced in academia.

Writing this book has been difficult but empowering. We decided on the word "unsettling" for its title because we want to disrupt the social relations of power and knowledge in universities and to question academic feminists' positions in and identifications with those relations. We are questioning ourselves as much as we are questioning others. We think that unsettling could contribute to politicizing and transforming the relations in the places where we have chosen to work as feminists. Not because we would *feel* better, but because we might become more accountable to a feminist politics inside and outside the university. And, as Himani shows in her essay, such a starting point could push us to re-examine and change feminist knowledge production and feminist theory.

Our work comes from the world we live in, as well as from the theories we use. We try to always move between one and the other, without saying "the" truth is in either; rather our interest lies in exploring how they rebound on each other. Because of this we have all written something which speaks to our personal lives, our political and our academic work. It surprised us that we took such similar approaches in our writing without prior consultation. In writing and talking about our work, we have come to regard each of the pieces and the collective manner in which the book has been produced as different examples of a critique which we'd like to see taken up more in feminist classrooms as well as in feminist texts.

Through locating and naming the practices we have been part of, we've faced questions and entered places where our efforts to write met strong boundaries. Because each piece reflects on where we are *located in* academic relations, we have felt vulnerable. We are located very differently — as student, part-time teacher, on limited contract or beginning tenure track appointments. None of us is speaking as a tenured faculty member. Moreover, as each essay shows, we have come to our current positions through very different avenues. In discussing and writing, we have disagreed, felt threatened, and have modified and edited what we've said along the way.

Each of the essays criticizes ways in which institutional practices "failed" us or other women, but the notion of unsettling goes beyond this. We're trying also to unsettle the places where we're comfortable, including unsettling the class, race and sexual relations of academic work. In some ways we're relatively comfortable in academia; part of the struggle is that we are quite "successful," and we want to understand the social relations and practices in which academic "success" and "failure" are produced. It is important for academic feminists to undertake such analysis now, especially in places where academic feminism has gained a certain legitimacy and where large numbers of feminist students bring a wide range of experience to bear on such analysis. This is the academic location which connects the five of us.

The way relations of power and knowledge are organized in and through the university makes it possible to live these relations without reflecting on them. This is especially the case for white, middle class, heterosexual men, but as more white, middle class, heterosexual women move into faculty and administrative positions, their/our centrality is so *obvious* that they/we don't even see them/ourselves as being central. Most often it takes another person to point out this centrality and the power and privileges it can confer; there is nothing from within the position that reflects back: it simply "is." This is how an unconscious non-naming can occur.

Naming the social construction of one's own power and privilege is quite different from talking about some other powerful group, with which we do not identify, as the oppressor. It is tempting for white, heterosexual, middle class women to name men as "the enemy" and to stop there. It is only another form of tokenism to produce work which allows a little space for class issues, a little space for differently-abled women, a little space for lesbians, a little space for non-white women, and so on, and then goes on very much as before. We have seen some students and colleagues become anxious and defensive about the questions we raise. We need to recognize that this is a racist, classist and heterosexist society and that the university is structured to perpetuate those relations. As feminists we need to examine our own different — and sometimes contradictory — locations in those relations.

We name the university as a place of feminist struggle. There has to be a way for privileged women working in academia to move beyond the personal blaming and feelings of guilt which often surround discussions of racism, homophobia, and so on. We do not want to disparage other feminists, but we think that political and theoretical critiques among feminists must include reflections on our own practices and locations. So, for example, we're not saying that all white women in academia are racist or that all heterosexual women are homophobic. We are saying that white middle class, heterosexual feminists who are in "comfortable" academic positions need to deconstruct the comfort and the power available to them. And, if those of us who are white, middle class and heterosexual can avoid getting bogged down in being offended by that, we can begin to ask, "Can I really step back, analyze this and find what it is that others are right about?" As Linda said to Kari in one of our meetings, "You don't have to try to feel what I feel, I don't want that. It's not about feeling. It's a political project."

We are not on socially undifferentiated ground: The power of some people is conditioned upon the powerlessness of others. The social relations that constitute power for one group are the flip side of that powerlessness. So, from different starting points and histories, and in different ways, we have come to realize that we need to see how the power of "normalcy" and non-naming reflects back, and how unself-consciousness can originate and be so easily perpetuated through the social relations of academia and by feminists working there, in spite of our best intentions.

The method we use to take up these questions reasserts self-questioning as a crucial analytical and political process. We also want to problematize the ways much of feminist theory has talked about "experience." Rather than taking it as an essentialist, static ground from which a woman's "identity" can be fixed and spoken about, we are talking about how experience (and identity) are social constructions in which we participate. What it is that we don't see about ourselves or that others don't see about us are the so-called normalcies. These are not normalcies in the biological sense but in the sense of having been defined as "normal" in ruling and discursive practices. This "not seeing" participates in the ruling practices which regulate the social relations in which we live. Historically, universities have been, and continue to be, central to the production and reproduction of such practices.

Many academic feminists now acknowledge differences among women and accept that white women cannot speak for non-white women. But perceiving the issue as just a matter of who can speak for whom can also offer a way out of dealing with the complexity of women's experience and women's oppression. It permits white women to forget about non-white women since "We have no right to speak for anyone but ourselves." This reading of the political and theoretical critiques of white feminism can be used to justify ignoring the majority of women in the world altogether. The very idea that anyone has to speak *for* someone else is a problem.

As women in academia we are or have been trained in certain kinds of discourse, certain kinds of disembodied ways of talking about the social and the individual. This works in many areas of feminist theory too. Woman as a category is taken up as if it weren't specific and located and historical. This way of thinking is embedded in the kind of training that we go through and the material and social settings in which it takes place. If we begin to look, we can see how the training works constantly to separate academic knowledge from actual people in actual classrooms with actual lives outside of those walls. This is also present in the writing, speech and interaction that are held up as scholarly when hirings take place and in the myriad structural patterns of the institutions in which the work actually goes on. And despite more women moving into those places, we worry that not much is changing, as feminist knowledge production in academia is beginning to construct its own orthodoxies around what counts as feminist scholarship. Even theorizing which is apparently critical and reflective of social relations often ignores the relations in which the writer is situated.

Academic training and knowledge production which ignore the social relations of the writer, teacher or student create the illusion of a common academic ground. This illusion claims, for example, that it doesn't matter that you live a lesbian life in a homophobic world or that you live in a racist society with black skin because we all come into this place together where, as Kate shows in her essay, the academic or scholarly problem is more likely to be defined as one of good and bad dichotomies than as actual relations of power and how to move them. It is possible to develop very sophisticated feminist theory without for a minute changing your own position in these relationships; it would probably be very good for your academic career to do so. But we have to wonder what kind of feminism we're producing if, no matter how brilliant the writing or the theory, the work that we do rests upon unexamined presuppositions about its disconnection from its location in everyday life and from political movements.

We are not using this book to expound on personal grievances, but rather to set up different points of view and to challenge dominant viewpoints. Like other feminists, we talk about these issues a lot, but how do we transcend them? We are struggling with the hows. And we don't pretend to have any final answer — it's a dialogue. We're working towards understanding and transforming the social relations in which academic feminists' work gets done. Although we often approach our own positions with ambivalence and with strong critiques, we think there are important struggles to be waged in universities. For us, these struggles are both personal and political.

# Black Women in Academia: A Statement from the Periphery

*by Linda Carty*

As a Black woman from the Caribbean, who attended university in this — a white — society, a heterosexual feminist activist, now referred to as an academic because I teach at university, I often reflect on the great gulf which exists between what I knew and know, what I was taught at university, what I actually learned and what I am now teaching.

I have sat in more classrooms than I care to remember where I had to listen to racist professors, both males and females, talk about a world that was always white and more often than not middle class. To have my very being negated on a daily basis in the academic enterprise soon taught me that not only was my presence not recognized, neither was my history. So it came as no surprise when, in a political science class discussion on African political traditions and economic development, the instructor boldly stated that history has shown us that Africans are not good managers of political power. According to him, they usually take state leadership positions and become despots because violence and barbarism are inherent features in their culture. When I questioned his assumptions and pointed to the pre-colonial African kingdoms with their well-established political institutions (which the imperial powers destroyed largely through violent means), his curt response was, "Tell us how many coup d'etats they've had in Nigeria since they gained political independence, or explain the barbaric crimes in Uganda and then tell us how these are related to colonialism, or perhaps you would prefer to wait and see what Mugabe and Nkomo will do with the Rhodesian economy a few years from now after they're given political control of that country." Needless to say, my instructor did not feel it incumbent upon him to explain Hitler's behaviour or Petain's or that of any number of European despots as inherent features of their culture.

Similarly, in one of the many oppressive English classes I felt forced to drop, the discussion was narrowly focussed on imagery in Joseph Conrad's *Heart of Darkness* and *The Secret Sharer*. When I dared to suggest that we look at Conrad's notion of "darkness" because, despite his seemingly progressive ideas, Conrad's reference to the Congo as the "heart of darkness" is clearly indicative of his own racialist views of Africa and its people, the professor calmly glanced in my direction and informed me that to read such meaning into the work is to miss the sophistication of Conrad's analysis and besides, "Africa with all its strange rituals and primitive cultures is understandably referred to as dark and not only by Conrad."[1] It did not occur to this purveyor of pure art that Conrad's analysis was childishly simple and that he had reached for the most handy, unanalytic and simplistic tools of racist common sense in his "literary" meandering.

After undertaking a comparative analysis of socialism in Cuba and in Manley's Jamaica for a sociology project, the professor informed me that the argument was so very lucid, the paper so well researched and written, that it was apparent to him that I must have received help with it since it would be rather difficult for a student at my level to present work of such calibre. Prior to this, I had never done a piece of work for him and he had never granted me an opportunity to speak in class. In other words, he had no evidence — if indeed evidence really mattered — on which to judge my capabilities. The implications of what he said, however, and more importantly, what he did not say, were as clear to me as they were to him.

None of these experiences was unique to me, even though

I was quite often the only Black student in a class or one of merely two or three. I would hear of similar experiences from other Black students on the campus. By all accounts, my experiences were commonplace among Black students. Perhaps what is even more chilling is that in discussions with young Black undergraduate students today, I realize that little has changed. Indeed, these experiences constitute Black students' place in the social relations of academia. This is the avenue through which I came to academia and it is the same avenue I continue to travel.

There is little difference between what we experience on the streets as Black women and the experiences we have inside the university. In both environments those experiences are structured by the same racist impulses and work to objectify and marginalize us. Within the university certain nuances and subtleties — the university's common sense appeal to reason and science — may take the rough edges off or sediment the particular behaviour, but the impact is no less severe.

The experience of being there and not being seen or acknowledged — the "outsider within" — is similar to the role which Georg Simmel calls the "stranger" in his essay on the sociological significance of such an outsider within (Georg Simmel, 1921: 322-27). It is the position of marginalization bell hooks describes Black women as occupying in the women's movement (bell hooks, 1984), and it is the same position which has, according to Patricia Hill Collins, provided Black women with "a special standpoint on self, family, and society." As Collins states: "Many Black intellectuals, especially those in touch with their marginality in academic settings, tap this standpoint in producing distinctive analyses of race, class, and gender" (Patricia Hill, 1986: S14-15). While there are definite benefits to be gained from the "outsider within" status, the drawbacks frequently outweigh the gains. As one author states: "For a time this marginality can be a most stimulating, albeit often a painful, experience. For some, it is debilitating ... for others, it is an excitement to creativity" (Alfred McClung Lee, 1973: 64).

Regardless, it leaves one perpetually tired from perpetual struggle.

In this paper, I address how the marginalization Black women experience in academia is created and show that the social relations of the academic world reflect the social world. Hence the relations of race, class and gender which work to keep Black women subordinated in the economy, for example, also keep them on the periphery in academia.

I discuss how knowledge claims which are legitimated through universities have predominantly been Eurocentric, white and male and therefore inherently gender-biased and racist. Similarly, other forms of knowledge are not recognized as valid because they contest these very bases. In my argument, I include some discussion of how feminism — although posing serious challenges to the social organization of knowledge — has, like "malestream" academic discourse, adequately addressed the issue of race. As a result, Black women are developing alternative epistemologies for dealing with their "outsider-within" status and these are challenging both feminist and mainstream knowledge claims.

## Historically Locating Black Women's Marginality

While there are many marginal groups within academia, women making up perhaps the most significant, as a Black feminist I have come to recognize that Black people in general, and Black women in particular, experience extreme marginality in the academic arena. In Canadian society, Black women, as a group, tend to experience their social world differently than do men and other women. In their relations with men, in the roles that are available to them in the family, in the labour market, in the paid and unpaid work that they perform, in their interactions with other women and in their knowledge of themselves, Black women's experiences are historically and institutionally structured in ways that are different from those who are not Black and female.[2]

Black women's experiences have been shaped by subordination. As a group they have been materially disadvantaged, a major feature of the subordination and victimization they experience because they are women and Black. But Black women have been more than victims; they have been actors, conscious builders of relations from which they can benefit, and though confined certainly to a very limited sphere of the white public patriarchal world, their very position affords them a clear understanding of their oppression. This allows them to be immersed in a world with positive merits which offers them the opportunity to be more than reactors to their "exclusion" from the white public patriarchal world (Gloria T. Hull et al. 1982).

Black women have been historically, and continue to be, active creators of their own world, where they play a significant role in shaping their immediate environment. Simultaneously they are objects of white male domination. These two seemingly contradictory roles are inextricably interwoven into a complex dialectic which cannot be ignored if the dynamic fuelling Black women's subordination is to be appreciated. To focus only on Black women's subordination and oppression is to undervalue their collective strength and resilience which have given rise to the alternative perspectives they have developed as most suitable for their reality. But to focus only on their historical strength as agents of change in their own world is to ignore the organized state and systemic oppression which impose severe limitations on their lives.

The history which Black women bring to academia is not recognized because academic discourse can only reflect the interests and concerns of its creators. As such, most theorizing about knowledge and the process of knowledge validation within this society's context has been Eurocentric, white and male. As Karl Mannheim rightly states: "If one were to trace in detail ... the origin and ... diffusion of a certain thought-model, one would discover the ... affinity it has to the social position of given groups and their manner of interpreting the world."[3] Eurocentric male dominance of academic discourse, then, has meant their constructing white as the reference point of all knowledge.

## Recognizing the Determinants of Academic Knowledge

As a Black woman sitting in a classroom in a white, advanced capitalist country where privilege usually translates into "white male," it was hardly accidental that the world was presented to me from that perspective, that is, a perspective in which I was an object of domination. What caused my questioning, however, was that this world was presented as everyone's reality, with no recognition or validity given to the knowledge of others who experience the world differently, or from a different standpoint, regardless (or perhaps because) of the experiential nature of that knowledge. What caused my questioning was that I had been taught, by my family since my birth, that white people existed in a world of privilege and that Black people's condition was in direct and opposing relation to that world. My family and my community had experienced the world through the paradigm of domination in which they stood invariably for the dominated. As Marx and Engels cogently argue:

> ...[D]efinite individuals who are productively active in a definite way enter into these definite social and political relations. Empirical observation must in each separate instance bring out empirically, and without any mystification and speculation, the connection of the social and political structure with production. The social structure and the State are continually evolving out of the life-process of definite individuals, not as they may appear in their own or other people's imagination, but as they *really* are: i.e. as they operate, produce materially, and hence as they work under definite material limits, presuppositions and conditions independent of their will (K. Marx and F. Engels, 1970: 46-47).

That people produce their conceptions and ideas based on their material experiences and history is correct. These conceptions and ideas become instruments of class struggle, class hegemony and the ruling social relations. Academia is and becomes a site of the "fashioning" of concepts, ideas, and values within the social relations.

Further, though the university is often a site of struggle where opposing views get aired, it is nevertheless a site of legitimation of the ruling social relations. As Ralph Miliband explains:

...[T]he pluralism and diversity which (universities) suggest are not quite as luxuriant as they might at first sight appear to be. For while universities are centres of intellectual, ideological and political diversity, their students are mainly exposed to ideas, concepts, values and attitudes much more designed to foster acceptance of the "conventional wisdom" than acute dissent from it. Many universities may harbour and make available to their students every conceivable current of thought; but everywhere too some currents are very much stronger than others (Miliband, 1969: 230).

The ruling class, which is constituted through the hegemony of white males, controls the knowledge production and validation process in this society. They set the terms and criteria for what will be recognized as valid social thought because they are located within the "community of experts" which is necessary to approve such thought and which is in the constant action of refuting and suppressing any other, under the veneer of pluralistic thought. It is easy, therefore, for this group to suppress or dismiss any other form of knowledge which may represent a challenge to its own. As Patricia Hill Collins aptly states:

Since the general culture shaping the taken-for-granted knowledge of the community of experts is one permeated by widespread notions of Black and female inferiority, new knowledge claims that seem to violate these fundamental assumptions are likely to be viewed as anomalies. Moreover, specialized thought challenging notions of Black and female inferiority is unlikely to be generated from within a white-male-controlled academic community because both the kinds of questions that could be asked and the explanations that would be found satisfying would necessarily reflect a basic lack of familiarity with Black women's reality (P. Hill Collins, 1989: 752).

The "community of experts," of which Collins speaks, gets its credibility from the larger society in which it is located because this is where its "taken-for-granted" knowledge originates. The significance of this is that even when a "community of experts" evolves out of the Black community its credibility (or lack of) is defined by white male hegemony. Presenting a challenge to this dominant group, therefore, means major obstacles for Black women scholars.

Thus, while Black women can produce knowledge claims that contest those advanced by the white male community, this community does not grant that Black women scholars have competing knowledge claims based in another knowledge-validation process. As a consequence, any credentials controlled by white male academicians can be denied to Black women producing Black feminist thought on the grounds that it is not credible research (P. Hill Collins, 1989: 753).

This has held true for much of the scholarship put forward by Black women and often by Black men. In my first year as a graduate student, I wrote a paper on colonialism and the possibility for socialist transformation in the English-speaking Caribbean. The professor for whom I had written the paper considered himself a "developmentalist" (his term). This meant he perceived himself as a specialist on *all* areas of the so-called developing world, be it Africa, Asia, Latin America or the Caribbean. He did not like my approach in the paper — marxist — neither did he approve of most of my sources, including the renowned Caribbean historian Eric Williams, who wrote the classic *Capitalism and Slavery*. "Furthermore," he said, "the Caribbean is a pluralist society, that's an irrefutable argument, so you should have read my article on that to give you an idea of how you should have approached such a topic." This was *my* world. I have been a victim of colonialism in that world, but he was not about to validate my knowledge claims derived largely through my experience or anyone else's that I chose to use from that world. That I did not use his article, that I did not construct my argument to his expectations meant that my analysis was invalid.

Often Black feminist scholarship receives a similar put down, as Collins points out, and sometimes this is at the hands of white feminists. Some years ago a fellow student did an analysis of stereotyped images of Black women. She stated that the dominant society has certain negative perceptions of Black women in particular which are fuelled by media stereotypes. The images of Black women on the television, for example, either as prostitutes, nursemaids (good nannies), or as loud, tough, single mothers, serve only to reinforce what the larger society regards as true. The professor on the course informed my friend that while it may have been true in the late sixties and early seventies that the media portrayed Black women in these negative roles, it is much less so today, and she cited the Bill Cosby show. While this particular professor's comments were hardly in support of racism, they were nevertheless without any basis in knowledge because those of us who are Black continue to see ourselves reflected in the media largely as criminals or idiots of one sort or another, exceptions not-withstanding, as the dominant stereotypes continue to be in-scribed over and over again.

The production and organization of knowledge by academicians linguistically and institutionally alienates Black women. Often the language used references the white upper-middle class world. It is often abstract since abstraction is part and parcel of the learned white male hegemonic discourse indicating academic knowledge. To articulate an alternative voice requires simultaneously comprehending the language of dominance and understanding the pervasiveness of the bureaucracy in the terrain to be contested. It is a seeing in which those who are marginalized succumb and resist simultaneously, their "identities are both created by the dominant discourse of power," while at the same time they continuously "create themselves in opposition to that discourse" (K.E. Ferguson, 1984: 22-23).

The resistance of such marginalized groups of individuals comes from an "outside knowledge" gained through experience, and a refusal to discard this, though it is not given legitimacy in the academic environment. In that environment, such groups as Black women, for example, do not regard academic knowledge as separate from and foreign to their everyday social world. Indeed, the social relations in both attempt to accomplish different results: in the academic environment it is the silencing and subordination of those who are made into objects, while in the experiential world it is a self-valuation and recognition of one's own power as a subject.

Black women's daily experiences with racism and sexism mean that their lives are less embedded in the linguistic and institutional hierarchical structures which define academia. The knowledge developed in this group — as with many other marginalized groups — does not depend solely on the dominant society's thought validation process, because it is knowledge which is used outside of and in opposition to the dominant society's domain and constitutes the everyday interactions of the group's social world. It is what Foucault refers to as "subjugated knowledges," which are "located low down on the hierarchy," far enough away from and sufficiently non-challenging to the mainstream that their "validity is not dependent on the approval of the established regimes of thought" (M.

Foucault, 1972: 81 & 82). It is this same knowledge, however, derived from their everyday experiences that Black women bring into the academic arena only to find that such knowledge forms are unacceptable.

Sitting as a subject in a class where the professor was objectifying me, I was also objectifying him. In our world as Black women we see him as the subject he presents to us and simultaneously as the object we know him to be. We come to know what he knows and at the same time to know him as we see him. In other words, we know the knowledge claims that he puts forward and what they represent and we know those knowledge claims to be incorrect in the face of what we know about the world.

The role of the professor in the classroom is that of arbiter of knowledge. But he cannot arbitrate our knowledge forms, though he may attempt to discredit them because they are outside of what he knows. So, as a Black woman, I entered the classroom knowing that what I was about to undertake was not something new about the world or something that would help me deconstruct any complexities in my own world. Instead, it was merely to learn the process of how the dominant knowledge forms are validated and given legitimacy for what counts as knowledge. This understanding is, of course, necessary for a Black woman if she hopes to negotiate and manoeuvre her way through academia.

## Black Women, the Ideology of Racism and Education

In academia, Black women's experience of education is determined by the assumed superiority of Eurocentric masculinist forms of knowledge. We can all remember, throughout our educational training, being as invisible in the texts as we were in the classroom discussions. White educators have always found it possible to write about life where Black people, like women in general, are not present or have had their roles subordinated. This invisibility assumes that the experience of white men is the norm for the entire population (A. Brittan and

M. Maynard, 1984:158). The experience of white men is understood as the experience which counts.

Another form that invisibility takes which is perhaps even more important is that of interpretations and explanations presented as objective — as if there were no possibility an alternative view could exist — when they represent white male understandings. An example of this is the claim that new world slavery was ended because it was a moral outrage to the progressive, kind-hearted white men who had assumed political power in Europe, instead of the recognition that slavery, with the perennial slave uprisings and sabotage, was less economically viable than the direct plunder of the countries from which slaves were taken. Similarly, colonialism and imperialism are presented as systems of Western philanthropy and benevolence — Christianizing the pagans and bringing modern "development" to backward societies — instead of systems of racism, cruelty, white supremacy and economic exploitation (A. Brittan and M. Maynard, 1984: 158). Such distortions and absences are indeed deliberate and are meant to deny the very essence of Black humanity as much as to make exploitation palatable. Furthermore, they promote racist and simplistic views and contribute to ignorance about the "non-white"[4] world. Such ideological misconceptions arise partly out of material comforts which, of course, serve as blinders to exploitation. Marx and Engels express this well, stating:

> The production of ideas, of conceptions, of consciousness, is at first directly interwoven with the material activity and the material intercourse of (sic) men, the language of real life. Conceiving, thinking, the mental intercourse of men, appear at this stage as the direct efflux of their material behaviour. The same applies to mental production as expressed in the language of politics, laws, morality, religion, metaphysics, etc. of a people. Men are the producers of their conceptions, ideas, etc. — real, active men, as they are conditioned by

a definite development of their productive forces and of the intercourse corresponding to these, up to its furthest forms. Consciousness can never be anything else than conscious existence, and the existence of men is their actual life-process (Marx and Engels, 1970: 47).

As Black people, we see our humanity being reduced to claims that we are populations of ignorant, uncivilized, lazy, childlike and illiterate peoples (A.Brittan and M. Maynard 1984:181), and we realize that uncovering and exposing the truth could take many generations. One author captures the issue of the negation of Black humanity well in his expose of how the African past was destroyed:

... [I]t is fair to say that the most significant of the obliterations of the New World's past was that which affected the African. The African became the more enduring "domestic enemy," and consequently the object around which a more specific, particular and exclusive conception of humanity was moulded. The "Negro," that is the colour black, was both a negation of African and a unity of opposition to white. The construct of Negro, unlike the terms African, Moor, or "Ethiope" suggested no situatedness in time, that is history, or space, that is ethno- or politico-geography. The Negro had no civilization, no cultures, no religions, no history, no place, and finally no humanity which might command consideration (C.J. Robinson, 1983:105).

Distortions of facts and the invisibility of peoples from the so-called "developing" and colonial world characterizes much of the learning by white students about the social world. Theirs has been a world in which whites are more privileged because it is assumed they are more intelligent, work harder and therefore their societies have advanced more rapidly. On the other hand, Black people as well as all peoples from that "developing" and colonial world, are shown as the architects of their own disadvantage. Both views represent a culture that is manufactured by and for those who benefit from sexism and racism.[5] It was hardly a surprise to me that I would often come out of a classroom with my white counterparts having a vastly different interpretation of a lecture we had all just heard. They would hear their reality and world view being reinforced and made alive because, after all, it was not a dead world the professor was referring to but a dynamic, continually advancing one. But I would not have heard even remote references to mine or would hear mine disparaged. Furthermore, whenever I bothered to disagree with the views presented in the lecture, this would be seen as a challenge to "the facts" and I would be perceived as "having an attitude problem." Translated this meant that I was not a team player because I was not prepared to accept and help maintain a culture which derides and excludes me because I am Black and female.

The way in which race, like sex, is socially constructed depends largely on a system of white male superiority and domination; it presupposes an ideology which takes the "reality" of race and sex for granted. Like all other forms of oppression, sex and race oppression are expressed and reproduced at the ideological level as though they were natural processes (Brittan and Maynard, 1984: 180). Furthermore, all forms of oppression involve the objectification of those being oppressed. It is the only way that oppression can actually work. In this case, the objectifying is primarily done by men who employ it as their basis of patriarchal power. They present the world which they have created as truth and objectivity but it is actually *their* world. Their power, then, is based on an ideology of masculinity which is "characterized by assumptions about potency of male subjectivity in a world of objects. From this point of view, masculinity is an ideology of domination" (A.Brittan and M.Maynard, 1984: 181). Similarly, on the issue of race, white subjectivity is held up as the norm, formulating a potent ideology by which everyone else is measured merely as objects. Again, there is an inextricable link between the material and ideological dimensions determining the essential constituents of knowledge.

For Black women in academia, mere survival means fighting this ideology on many levels. While all women must fight against the ideological discourse of sexism, Black women must struggle additionally against the ideological discourse of racism. So that while the former can choose to do battle only against male domination (as many white middle class women do), for the latter, the struggle by necessity includes men and society at large. As Michele Wallace rightly asserts:

> We exist as women who are Black who are feminists ... working independently because there is not yet an environment in this society remotely congenial to our struggle — because, being on the bottom, we would have to do what no one else has done: we would have to fight the world (M. Wallace, 1982: 12).

The ideology of domination manifests itself in many ways which encourage people to accept unquestioningly the myths and beliefs about the social world. This too is a form of knowledge based on what some authors have referred to as "common sense" — it is taken as what we all "know," it can be exaggerated and distorted, but is largely accepted by all as representing:

> ...the distilled truths of centuries of practical experience; so much so that to say of an ideal or practice that it is only common sense, is to appeal over the logic and argumentation of intellectuals, to what all reasonable people know in their "heart of hearts" to be right and proper. Such an appeal can act at one and the same time to foreclose any discussion about certain ideas and practices and to legitimate them (E. Lawrence, 1982: 48).

The common sense notion has a built-in contradiction in that it does not have an inherent logic, nor does it constitute a unified body of knowledge. While it "embodies the practical experience and solutions to the everyday problems encountered by the 'popular masses' throughout their history, it is also shot through with elements and beliefs derived from earlier or other more developed ideologies which have *sedimented* into it" (E. Lawrence, 1982: 49). Common sense knowledge then is often oppositional and always contradictory. Yet because it appeals to the larger society without demanding any intellectualizing for its notions to be legitimized, ideology which can be transmitted as common sense is beneficial to those in control of the relations of ruling. For example, most people make their decisions about issues of race and gender based on their common sense knowledge.[6] But we do know there is the ruling ideology which fosters and perpetuates female subordination and Black inferiority. However, because this is something which "everyone knows" — i.e., that women are to be treated as subordinate to men and Blacks as inferior to whites — it is not regarded as an ideology of state practice. Common sense knowledge therefore makes inequality and discrimination appear natural (Brittan and Maynard, 1984:182).

Ideology is a constituitive element which constructs a range of social experiences in people's everyday interactions. It "is not simply imposed from the outside by some super-powerful socialization agency; on the contrary, it is used by people to define their own lives and to understand the struggles and conflicts of the world they live in" (Brittan and Maynard, 1984:183). It also does not exclude exceptions, though the exceptions never manage to break through or break down what is defined as the norm. On the contrary, the exceptions work to legitimize the norms. Thus, when, for example, the state evicts Black single mothers from subsidized housing, claiming that such action is necessary because these women allow their sons to traffic in drugs in the housing projects, people claim to "understand" that the government, the police and the courts are really trying to reduce criminal and drug activity in Toronto and to keep the city safe. Hence they are doing what is necessary to protect the larger society. It is easier to see Blacks as innately criminal than it is to see racism on the part of the state or to see the failure on the part of the government to provide employment for disadvantaged youths.

Similarly, when Black students are streamed into the lowest levels of the educational system, where Black teenage girls are forced to take up hairdressing or nurse's aides courses as their only potential employment, their motivation is stripped from them, their goals destroyed, and a menial job becomes their only destiny. Consequently they become frustrated and angry, engage in acts of resistance and are then labelled "antisocial" and "lacking in ambition" by the dominant society. The common sense ideology is that Blacks are not academically inclined. This was presumed in the first instance as part of the ideology of racism and was responsible for the act of streaming. These are some of the ways in which common sense images of Black people are formulated. They are always tied to a common sense racist ideology which refers to *all* Black people.

Racism and sexism are products of the same discursive world. They are both characterized by the process of objectification. Furthermore, racism as an ideology permeates all aspects of society, transcending class and knowledge claims. It is not only applied by those in power in relations of ruling, but also manifests itself as an ideology of common sense and of experience in the larger society. It is characterized by notions people carry around in their heads and act upon without reflecting on them, by seemingly unconscious ways of thinking and acting (Brittan and Maynard, 1984:184-185).

**The Derision of Black Humanity in Academic Discourse**
Though racism and sexism are socially constructed by the same process of objectification, in white feminist theory racism takes on a life of its own which closely resembles the way it is played out ideologically in the wider society. That is, racism is ideologically accepted by most white feminist theorists, even when their stated intent is to struggle along side "non-white" women against sexism. Hence in most feminist analyses of oppression,

every other form of oppression is made secondary to sexism or at least sexism is seen as essential and discrete. While it is now widely accepted that racism compounds the problem of sexism for Black women, few white feminists have looked seriously at the issue of race and how it intersects with gender. As far as undertaking an analysis of women's oppression, gender has largely been examined as a discrete category — distinct from race and class. This has serious implications for how feminist theory intends to redress the wrongs men have heaped on women by excluding them from academic discourse. More specifically, Elizabeth Spelman rightly argues:

> If feminism is essentially about gender, and gender is taken to be neatly separable from race and class, then race and class don't need to be talked about except in some peripheral way. And if race and class are peripheral to women's identities as women, then racism and classism can't be of central concern to feminism. Hence the racism and classism some women face and other women help perpetuate can't find a place in feminist theory unless we keep in mind the race and class of all women (not just the race and class of those who are the victims of racism and classism) (E. Spelman, 1988:112).

Indeed, it is essential to analyze race and class not only in the context of racism and classism in interaction with sexism, but also within the category of gender. That is, to examine how race and class are played out in gender as a social construct. Yet even serious-minded marxist feminists, who bring a historical materialist approach to their inquiry, fail to make these important connections, just as marxists fail to see how race is manifested within class. Nancy Hartsock, for example, in her highly acclaimed work on "the feminist standpoint," fails to theorize race and class into her analysis.[7] Instead, she pays lip service[8] to differences in women's experiences based on race and class, but refuses to acknowledge the implications of these differences and goes right on theorizing sexism as separate from and independent of race and class oppression.[9] As many Black, South Asian, Native, and Asian feminists have long stated, we do not share any common experience of oppression with white women from which it could be possible to theorize "a feminist standpoint" and assume a unity of social relations in feminism. As a Black woman, my sisters and I continually discuss this problematic and find it ludicrous that seemingly well-intentioned feminists like Hartsock cannot (or are unwilling to) understand that we cannot be female *or* Black, we *are* female *and* Black. For us the two are one and the same, we do not have a choice. As Black women we experience our femaleness and Blackness together, always at the same time, and we challenge whether it is possible for white women to be white *or* female because we see them as white *and* female.

The position Hartsock and other marxist feminists have taken on the "women's standpoint" is not new. A similar argument is advanced by Kate Millett in her *Sexual Politics* back in 1969, and by Shulamith Firestone in *The Dialectic of Sex*, one year later. Like Hartsock and other contemporary feminist theorists, both authors advance the view that sexism is the more endemic oppression, reducing race and class to sex. What is disturbing about this is that the position is itself racist; it obscures the white middle class feminist authors' role as oppressors at numerous social moments of other women and, in this case, of Black men. Furthermore, these theorists presume to speak for all women by dismissing the very potent social relations of race and class as organizing principles in so many women's lives. Like white middle class men before them, these feminist theorists have assumed a legitimacy which has been obtained through the oppression of other women. In doing so, they attempt to strive for a commonality among women, but what they accomplish is a stand of authority and superiority. And as Spelman poignantly states, we ought to scrutinize such analyses which emphasize women's commonality because:

... however logically, methodologically, and politically sound such inquiry seems, it obscures the ways in which race and class identity may be intertwined with gender identity. Moreover, since in a racist and classist society the racial and class identity of those who are subject to racism and classism are not obscured, all it can really mask is the racial and class identity of white middle-class women. It is because white middle-class women have something at stake in not having their racial and class identity made and kept visible that we must question accepted feminist positions on gender identity (E. Spelman, 1988:112).

The point, as bell hooks states, is that "certainly it has been easier for women who do not experience race or class oppression to focus exclusively on gender" (bell hooks, 1984:14).

In reiterating this debate we are reminded of Audre Lorde's statement: "how difficult and time-consuming it is to have to reinvent the pencil every time you want to send a message" (Audre Lorde, 1984:78). Each time we want to discuss feminism and our struggle as Black women in a white society, it is necessary to deal with feminist theories which promote women's commonalities while ignoring their differences, in other words, with what Adrienne Rich calls "white solipsism." According to Rich, this is "the tendency 'to think, imagine, and speak as if whiteness described the world.' "[10] Similarly, one has to go through all the arguments about academic knowledge claims which are perpetuated by white male academicians before getting to the knowledge and experience of Black people. However, it is necessary to expose such theories for two reasons. First, they suggest that Black women have to choose being women over being Black or choose being women and not being Black. Second, as a corollary to the first, this means I have to relocate myself as a Black woman, as a feminist who rightfully demands that my voice be heard in this debate.

It is not only within this debate that I demand a voice but

against all racists, even those who are feminists. This fight is exhausting. It is a daily occurrence whether we are merely walking down the street while racial epithets are hurled at us or whether we are travelling the seemingly sterilized halls of academia where, though such actions may be muted, the message is nevertheless the same. In academia, of course, it means being on the periphery though supposedly being on the inside.

When I started this paper I recounted some of my experiences in order to locate myself as a Black woman in a white society and in the academic terrain. It is impossible for a Black feminist to present any kind of analysis without employing an historical location of Black people in advanced capitalist society as the point of departure. It is absolutely necessary that we do this, as the reader cannot appreciate our individual positions without getting a sense of our collective location. The political is of necessity personal for us. I have found writing this paper rather difficult, not only because I believed for a long time, as I had been schooled, that the personal (as in *I* the subject) has no place in "real" academic discourse — after all, the medium we were told, is neutral. Nevertheless, those of us who are not white, male and affluent are always identified by our race, class and gender. So much for learned neutrality. But it is also because I am unable to fathom a separation between that *I* and the collective history from which it originates. And as I read over what I have already written, I realize that this is manifested in my usage of *I*, *me* and *our* interchangeably. This, reflects both collective thinking and the attempt at self location, while simultaneously attempting not to construct this debate as a personal debacle because that it certainly is not. I do recognize, however, that feminism as a theory and political process requires that we analyze the subjectivity we have had constructed for us as women in order to break down the social construction of gender within the patriarchal world of capitalism. In continuing to do this, I will now explicate some of what I mentioned at the beginning of the paper in order to point out that what is being contested through racism and sexism in academia is Black humanity itself.

As I listened to professors deride Africa and African peoples around the world either overtly or implicitly again and again, I experienced profound anger and a sense of powerlessness. It was then that I began realizing how university-based knowledge claims are produced and reproduced. While such claims are socially constructed and open to political struggle, they are continually passed off as legitimate because the very milieu in which they are socially constructed negates contestation. That is, in the larger world, the factors which facilitate the construction of such knowledge claims are themselves built on the assumed inferiority of others, in this case that of peoples of African origin.

Since being brought to the West some five hundred years ago, Black people have had to struggle to maintain our humanity. The intensity of the struggle may have abated on some levels, now that we are moving into the twenty-first century, and our resistance has proven the assumptions about us incorrect. But struggle is still very much needed. It is not that our humanity or history is now accepted or understood. Indeed, far from it, many of the assumptions are now institutionalized practice, employed regularly by those who have gained the power to dominate academic discourse.

It is rather difficult to see how, out of a history of racialism and the disparagement of Blacks by the Eurocentric, male power structure within academia, anything else could emerge without our continued struggle. Indeed, this disparagement of African peoples is itself a construct of the social relations of capitalism, which we must continue to fight. The history of struggle and resistance by African peoples is succinctly stated by Cedric Robinson in the following quote, which is presented in its entirety to capture the essence of the issue — what he refers to as the emergence of the "Black radical tradition":

For some 400 years, from the 15th to the 19th Century, while the capitalist mode of production in Europe engulfed agrarian and artisanal workers, transforming them over the generations into expropriated, dependent fodder for concentration in factories, disciplined to the rhythms and turbulances of the manufacturing process, the organizers of the capitalist world system appropriated Black labour power as *constant* capital. Blacks were extracted from their social formations through mechanisms which, by design and historical coincidence, minimized the disruption of the production of labour. ... For those African men and women whose lives were interrupted by enslavement and transportation, it was reasonable to expect that they would attempt, and in some ways realize, the recreation of their lives. It was not, however, an understanding of the Europeans which preserved those Africans in the grasp of slavers, planters, merchants and colonizers. Rather, it was the ability to conserve their native consciousness of the world from alien intrusion, the ability to imaginatively recreate a precedent metaphysic while being subjected to enslavement, racial domination and repression. This was the raw material of the Black radical tradition, the values, ideas, conceptions and constructions of reality from which resistance was manufactured. And in each instance of resistance, the social and psychological dynamics which are shared by human communities in long-term crises resolved for the rebels the particular moment, the collective and personal chemistries which congealed into social movement. But it was the materials constructed from a shared philosophy developed in the African past and transmitted as a culture, from which revolutionary consciousness was realized and the ideology of struggle formed (C.J. Robinson, 1983:442-443).

This is the historical and cultural origin of Blacks in the West. Resistance, therefore, is a necessity.

As I sat in the many social science classes where instructors, through their actions and/or their words, continually constructed a world in which Blacks were inferior to whites, and presented this as a given, an awareness of this history allowed me to contain my anger and pain. At the level of university education, resistance by the victims of this type of racism is hardly ever expected. Those expounding the distorted knowledge claims perceive themselves as engaged in the "correct" and "factual" production of knowledge, and often even those who know differently fail to object. For example, in the political science class mentioned earlier, though there were two Black male graduate students sitting in on the course, they did not challenge the professor all year, nor did they support me when I did. Yet they would come to me after class to let me know that I had their support. The problem with this type of behaviour is that it was exactly what was expected of us and contributed directly to making us non-persons in the classroom.

Furthermore, it indicated to me the uniqueness of Black women's struggle. Not only do we have to address the oppression we experience as women by whites, but often we have to work separately from Black men because, though we share a great deal as victims of racism, patriarchy allows them certain privileges which we are denied. Whatever those privileges were perceived to be by my male counterparts in that class, they were not about to risk them by getting on the "wrong side" of the professor, as I clearly did. Since they were being supervised in their graduate work by the same professor, they were in that class for one reason, to fulfill his expected wishes. Surely it was not lost on them that obtaining a doctoral degree would confer upon them a certain kind of power relative to me and most other Blacks, whether in this society or in their country of origin. Hence it was very clear to them what role they were expected to play, and even though it involved some negation of the self, patriarchy gave them a closer affinity to the professor than to me.

I dared to challenge professors in courses such as sociology and political science because at least in these disciplines one is given the impression that there is room for debate. Theories are in a seemingly continuous process of evolution. In other disciplines, it is very apparent there is no room for debate. In English, for example, most of what gets into the classroom is culled from the European literary tradition, from the Victorian epoch particularly — the time of the colonial expansion of empire. Knowledge claims of that period are presented as established order in a clearly unquestioning framework. So that even though my first interest in university was English, since I mistakenly believed that one could *learn* to be a writer through this study, it quickly became apparent to me that unless I was prepared to accept that all the females in the texts were "ladies" because they were white, that all the white men were intelligent and therefore powerful, and that any Blacks would always be portrayed as "primitive," and further accept that this is so because, as one white teaching assistant tried to assure me, "art merely imitates life, but don't take these things so personally," I realized I would hardly survive.

### Feminist "Underdevelopment": Gender Without Race and Class

My undergraduate experiences in the classroom differed somewhat from my experiences as a graduate student, that is, so far as encountering ignorance born out of racism almost on a daily basis. This is not to suggest that racism was not apparent in graduate school, only that it was more subtle, making the experience somewhat more "liveable." Indeed, the social relations of the environment were still determined and defined by racial assumptions. As a graduate student, I perceived having more autonomy over my academic life, and in the department in which I studied, beyond the course work and other administrative requirements, students are completely free to develop their own programs. I liked this aspect of things, though I later realized that this was due to my very independent-minded personality, developed through my early family teachings in life. Had I been a student who expected or needed constant guidance, or even encouragement, my experience would have surely been different.

Besides, being a student without financial support meant that I had to work throughout my post-secondary education, often times doing both on a full-time basis. In graduate school this was not unusual for most of the "non-white" students, especially those of us who were "fortunate" enough not to be designated as foreign students. Now, in my post-student life, I often wonder how I managed to work, be fairly active in departmental student politics, remain actively involved in my community and still complete my doctoral studies in average time.

As other authors in this collection also state, the department of sociology at OISE, University of Toronto, has a strong feminist orientation. We can easily get the illusion that a feminist consciousness will contribute to a more palatable environment, if only through some sense of sharing gender subordination. Feminism, after all, is pertinent to grasping the workings of patriarchal power relations. However, I found that this was hardly the case.

It is not an exaggeration to say that in the department feminism constitutes the primary political and academic discourse among both faculty and students. The department produces the largest number of feminist dissertations in the entire university. Most of the women who enter the department as new graduate students do so to pursue work in feminist studies. The department attracts many feminist activists and women who are interested in developing a critical understanding of power relations and women's subordination.

When I started graduate work at OISE I would not have identified myself as a feminist. I considered myself a Black nationalist and marxist, having closely followed the work and teachings of the Black Power Movement in the United States and Toronto in the early seventies, and later pursuing formal studies in marxism independently and as an undergraduate student. In my association with some Black organizations in Toronto in the days of the Black Power Movement, I do remember getting fairly disgusted with the subordinate roles I saw women either willingly taking on or being forced to occupy. However, I did not have the tools to help me in articulating or analyzing this.

My awareness of gender inequality, however, and my desire to understand the social relations of this phenomenon brought me to the study of feminism. Observing the politics (or lack thereof) of feminism, by some self-identified feminist faculty who taught courses in women's studies and also by some students who proudly identified themselves as feminists, aroused my interest in the particular study of feminism as political praxis and academic discourse.

I perceived little difference between the women who identified themselves as feminists and those who did not in their reactions to me in and out of classes when I raised the issue of racism within feminism. Furthermore, I had two direct encounters with a feminist professor who was quite overt in expressing her racism. I also had to sit in classes and listen while terms like "primitive" were thrown around loosely, always in reference to Blacks and/or pre-capitalist societies — whether this was in reference to Marx's primitive accumulation theory, which was not adequately explored, or in studying Hegel without addressing his racist dismissing of peoples of Africa.[11]

By this time, I had long concluded that orthodox marxism did not hold the answers for us Black women because it fails to address race and gender, and in my dismissal of radical and liberal feminism for their imperviousness to racism I was also forced to reassess the relevance of marxist feminism which, although it has gone much further than any previous theoretical paradigm in analyzing class and gender, has also failed to theorize race into its analysis (H. Hartman, 1979; Z. Eisenstein, 1979; M. O'Brien 1981; N. Hartsock, 1983, M. Barrett, 1983; L. Vogel, 1983, etc.).

My working in feminism was not merely in a university setting or through a theoretical knowledge, however. At the same time I was — and still am — a member of a very politically active Black women's collective and have been an activist in our community as a counsellor and literacy worker. It was through my community work that I really learned the difference between feminist theory and its praxis and came to appreciate that difference and realized that feminism too will fail to have an impact upon the social world in which most women exist, unless those of us doing the theorizing really make attempts to understand that world. It is in this everyday world that most working class women find the state, for example, working against them, through the problems they encounter with employment, childcare, etc. It is in this everyday world that most "non-white" women find racism compounding these problems.[12] Feminist theory which continues not to analyze race and class in sexism has to be dismissed as inadequate and irrelevant to most women's lives.

As a Black woman now teaching university in a society where this is extremely rare, I am aware, like the few other "non-white" women in a similar position, of the unique opportunity I now have to redress some of the historical inaccuracies perpetrated by Eurocentric scholars, including feminists, who refuse to recognize the changing nature of the social world. When I stand in front of virtually all-white classes in a university that hardly reflects the very diversified racial and ethnic make up of the city, attempting to discuss the implications of colonialism, imperialism and their connections to racism, and have to listen to students tell me that "non-whites" who come to Canada should be grateful to the government because they are *given* the opportunity to become much better off in every way than they could ever have been in their country of origin, or have to listen to white women who believe that my teaching in the university reflects the strides feminism and "non-white" women are making, I realize how much work there is to be done and how much I can contribute.

The opportunity presents an exciting challenge for "non-white" women bringing our feminist praxis inside the university. We have a regular audience which we could not otherwise encounter on a daily or even weekly basis. We are aware also of the attempts to contain our efforts. Indeed, our marginalization is no accident but neither is our politics of coalition with those white feminists we have found who are prepared to risk the power accorded them by virtue of their race and class. They are still far too few, but our joint effort is the only road forward which guarantees any prospect for constructive social change.

## Endnotes

1. Perhaps it ought not be a surprise then that almost fifteen years later, the Royal Ontario Museum mounted a controversial exhibition looking at Canadian missionaries' role in Africa during the colonial era dubiously entitled *Into the Heart of Africa*, which many find riddled with racist assumptions and connotations. The exhibition presented Africa and the history of the African peoples from the perspective of the missionaries.

2. These differences have been structured by race, class and gender relations. See Paula Giddings *When and Where I Enter: The Impact of Black Women on Race and Sex in America*, New York: William Morrow, 1984; and Jacqueline Jones *Labour of Love, Labour of Sorrow: Black Women, Work and the Family from Slavery to the Present*, New York: Basic Books, 1985, for in depth analyses of Black women's experiences in this context.

3. Karl Mannheim, *Ideology and Utopia: An Introduction to the Sociology of Knowledge*, New York: Harcourt Brace, 1936, p. 276. With regard to tracing the origin of the tendency for western scholarship to invalidate Black people's history and culture, fabricating national myths which have constituted the tools of class

hegemony, see Cedric Robinson, *Black Marxism: The Making of the Black Radical Tradition*, London: Zed Press, 1983 particularly chap. 9.

4. I use this term being fully cognizant that it assumes peoples and/or regions have homogeneous experiences and/or cultural identities. It is certainly not the intent here to reduce our diversity or rich differences to some kind of commonality (which could be misconstrued as nothingness, i.e., that those who are not white have no independent identities.) The term as used here is to be taken literally, merely meaning "other than."

5. See Dorothy Smith *The Everyday World as Problematic*, Toronto: University of Toronto Press, 1987, especially Chapter 1, "A Peculiar Eclipsing: Women's Exclusion from Man's Culture," for an argument of how men create what is legitimate as culture, and how though manufactured for women also, it is entirely male because it totally excludes women. A similar argument can be applied regarding race.

6. I am referring to whites on the issue of race and whites and Blacks on the issue of gender. Common sense knowledge is arrived at in the same manner by all groups but, of course, it is applied only to what is non-offensive to that particular group.

7. Nancy Hartsock, "The Feminist Standpoint: Developing the Ground for a Specifically Feminist Historical Materialism," in *Discovering Reality: Feminist Perspectives on Epistemology, Metaphysics, Methodology and Philosophy of Science*, pp. 283-310, Sandra Harding and Merrill B. Hintikka, eds. Holland: D. Reidel, 1983. For a cogent critique of Hartsock, see Marlee Kline, "Women's Oppression and Racism: A Critique of the 'Feminist Standpoint,' pp. 37-64 in *Race, Class, Gender: Bonds and Barriers*, Socialist Studies 5, Toronto: Between the Lines, 1989. Others who promote a feminist standpoint include Hilary Rose, "Hand, Brain and Heart: A Feminist Epistemology for the Natural Sciences," *Signs*, Vol. 9, 1983.

8. She states throughout her analysis that we must recognize difference not merely at a level of tolerance but recognize its "creative function."

9. As bell hooks points out, socialist feminists often make a point of acknowledging the importance of race, for example, then go right on to present an argument in which race is absent. *Feminist Theory: From Margin to Centre*, p. 14.

10. Adrienne Rich as quoted in Spelman, p. 116.

11. Typical of many of the scholars of his time, Hegel, in his discussion of African peoples freely expresses perceptions which could only have been based on ignorance. In his introduction to *The Philosophy of History*, he says:

> The peculiarly African character is difficult to comprehend, for the very reason that in reference to it, we must quite give up the principle which naturally accomplishes all *our** ideas — the category of Universality. In Negro life the characteristic point is the fact that consciousness has not yet attained to the realization of any substantial objective existence — as for example, God, or Law — in which the interest of man's volition is involved and in which he realizes his own being. This distinction between himself as an individual and the universality of his essential being, the African in the uniform, undeveloped oneness of his existence has not yet attained; so that the Knowledge of an absolute Being, an Other and a Higher than his individual is entirely wanting. The Negro, as already observed, exhibits the natural man in his completely wild and untamed state. We must lay aside all thought of reverence and morality — all that we call feeling — if we would rightly comprehend him; there is nothing harmonious with humanity to be found in this type of character. The copious and circumstantial accounts of

Missionaries completely confirm this... p. 93
* Hegel's emphasis.

This is not a suggestion that academic feminists become community activists, but surely, feminism as a political process demands more than a footnote as an awareness of this world.

# Leaving the Comfort of Home: Working through Feminisms

## by Kari Dehli

In this paper I talk about academic feminism and my own participation in it. I weave together four stories: the first is about some features of feminist knowledge production in academe and how we might talk about them; the second is the story of how I became an academic feminist; the third is about a thesis and a paper I wrote and re-wrote; and the fourth story is about my mother and my memories of childhood in Norway. Through these intersecting stories I hope to understand better how feminism gets done as academic practice and how that practice might be done differently. Since much of what I am describing comes from my own memories and from thinking about the work that I do, writing this has forced me to face some unsettling questions about my own, changing positioning as an "academic feminist," and as a white, middle class, heterosexual and able-bodied woman in Canadian society and in feminist politics.

## The First Story

As I have worked on this paper, and as we have worked together as a group on this book, I have thought more about the tensions in, and implications of, the processes of identification and identity formation. It has been important for individual women and for many women's movements proudly and defiantly to claim a positive identity as women, rejecting the negative identifying practices of dominant social institutions and discourses. Nevertheless, like others, I have trouble with the assumed fixed-ness and often ahistorical character of the categories feminists use to identify ourselves and each other (Riley 1988), and with the ways that the category "woman" glosses over differences among women (Spelman 1988; hooks 1984). Recent critical writings on difference and identity, autobiography and post-structuralism, have claimed new spaces for "the personal" in feminist theory while challenging assumptions of the unitary, coherent and stable subject "Woman" prevalent in much earlier feminist writing (Adams 1989; Steedman 1986; de Lauretis 1990). Some of these writers take feminist knowledge production within academia as their problematic, but they do so without resorting to arguing that academic feminism is "bad" because the women who do it are mostly white, middle class and heterosexual. Instead, they want to understand the social relations and material conditions within which such knowledge is produced. They analyze relations of power in the academy, and the ways in which women are positioned (differently) in those relations (Smith 1990). While insisting on the social organization of knowledge and of knowledge production, they leave room for politics and for change.

Thinking in terms of changing locations and of the multiplicity of experience offers a way of analyzing how those of us who are "inside" the powerful social relations of academic feminism can work within and resist the trappings of comfort and "home-ness" which it appears to offer. It continues to be the case that most women and most feminists working in Canadian universities find themselves in departments that are at best tolerant of, and at worst hostile to, feminism (Smith 1987b; Eichler 1990). Thus, it is important to keep in mind that even though some feminists may be "insiders" in universities, they are by no means at the centre (Harlow 1989). They continually struggle in and against institutional structures which undermine feminist knowledge and feminist methodology.

Feminists need theory in order to understand the social

relations of academic knowledge production and women's different positions in them. As a project of politics and theory-building, feminism has been central to the work of critiquing dominant power relations, including dominant forms of knowledge and practices of knowledge production (Harding and Hintikka 1983; Smith 1990). We can construct more theoretically adequate and politically self-conscious accounts of the social relations of sex and gender, and the formation of "identities" if, when we construct theory, we consider our own as well as others' personal histories of positioning in social relations. Although I am sceptical toward some of the uses and implications of post-structuralism, I agree with many other feminists that its strategies of deconstruction and notions of multiple subjectivities and shifting locations are helpful in grappling with questions of "difference" and "othering" (Chow 1989; Spivak 1985; Walkerdine 1987). Nevertheless, in the face of much post-structuralist writing I often feel quite frankly intimidated and dazzled. The language is so clever, so witty — but what is it about? Sometimes I feel like an intruder into a domain for which I have not been properly initiated. Growing up in Norway and not learning the "canons" of English literature does not help, since so much of post-structuralist writing takes the form of literary criticism. But, it is more than this that makes me feel uneasy as many academic feminists (and marxists) eagerly embrace notions that all the world is a text open to an infinity of deconstructions and multiple readings. I want to put such notions together with the systematically organized conditions in which the majority of the world's women labour to provide for themselves and for their children, with the very systematic ways in which rape and violence are inflicted on women, as well as with the myriad of ways in which women subvert, organize and resist oppression. I'm not sure that reading the world as a text (as post-structuralists recommend) leads to the conclusion that all the world *is* a text. Nor do I think that all the world's problems can be grasped by textual, deconstructive strategies or how such intellectual strategies may (or may not) be grounded in feminist politics. For example, it is paradoxical that some women's ability to pursue infinite deconstructions (feminist or otherwise) of "truth" or "narrative" in North American universities is predicated upon the socially organized, international division of labour. Moreover doing academic work "properly" depends upon a radical separation of mind and body, upon repressing, for example, feelings of fear and desire or memories of sexual violence (Rockhill 1987). Perhaps it is possible to take up some of the tools of post-structuralism without abandoning theory and empirical and historical grounding of politics, and without forgetting our bodily knowing.

This paper begins to work through these questions. It is an unfinished paper, rewritten, many times and shaped by the ideas and observations of many other people, some of whom are the co-authors of this book.[1] My ideas have also been stimulated by reading, an activity I have been able to pursue as a graduate student. Two articles have been especially important for this paper. I have read and re-read Minnie Bruce Pratt's essay "Identity: Skin Blood Heart"(1984) and Biddy Martin and Chandra Talpade Mohanty's analysis of it, "Feminist Politics: What's Home Got to Do with It?" (1986). A white lesbian feminist in the United States, Pratt charts her difficult and ever-changing journey to situate herself in relation to the places she has lived and the people around her. This journey is one where she never settles down in a stable and comfortable identity. It is rather a moving through and a remembering of unstable locations and of people in them. Pratt is critical of attempts to build the trappings of home around feminism, even as she acknowledges her desire for familiarity and security. For me, her story points to the unsettling realization that any "comfort of home" within feminism (or elsewhere) for middle class, white feminists in a classist, racist, sexist and heterosexist North American society, is predicated on exclusion, denial, oppression and violence. But Pratt does not take on the categories defining identity — skin, blood, heart — as essential, fixed and stable.

Instead, she takes us through a journey of self-reflection and changing location, thus leaving room for hope and possibility for feminist politics. It is this theme in her essay that Martin and Mohanty explore. They write:

> What we have tried to draw out of this text is the way in which it unsettles not only any notion of feminism as an all-encompassing home but also the assumption that there are discrete, coherent, and absolutely separate identities — homes within feminism, so to speak — based on absolute divisions between various sexual, racial, or ethnic identities.... The "unity" of the individual subject, as well as the unity of feminism, is situated and specified as the product of the interpretation of personal histories; personal histories that are themselves situated in relation to the development within feminism of particular questions and critiques.(1986:192)

Now that I have told you about these two articles, I realize that "referring to the literature" is a way of saying: This is the frame through which I want you to read and think about the paper. Referring to Pratt, Martin and Mohanty is pertinent in as much as the questions they raise are similar to ones I want to address. But it is only because I have been able to spend most of my time over the past ten years studying that I even know about this kind of writing, let alone how to read it. Learning particular forms of argument — debating within new or established academic discourses — is an important part of academic training. Through university training, feminists too learn to become competent in it. Becoming competent and confident within this sort of knowledge production and circulation — feeling "at home" in it — can become a double-bind for feminists, however. The pressures to write, research or teach within specific forms, for example, by showing "mastery" of "the literature," are embedded in the ways university education is put together and practiced. Learning how to use difficult concepts, reciting the arguments of "great" theorists, or publishing in scholarly journals is a hard and time-consuming business. It is this kind of work rather than political activism and personal history which counts as properly academic. The more feminists adjust their work to these parametres, the more we risk being split from transformative politics within and beyond the universities (Evans 1986; Eichler 1990).

What is left out of much academic feminist knowledge production is not just political activism but self-conscious and politically self-critical reflections of the kind that Pratt has written, or — I should be more specific here — the kind of account that Pratt has produced is not uncommon among non-white, working class or lesbian feminists, writing in and out of academic settings about the centrality of skin, blood and heart to their lives and to their feminism (see other chapters in this book). But why is it so rare for white, middle class and heterosexual feminists in the university to place ourselves in this kind of writing? This has partly to do with the pressures I've described above, to be sure. But there seems also to be another process at work here, even as academic feminists embrace autobiography and personal narratives. While it is important for all kinds of women to tell stories of relations with men and experiences in male-dominated institutions, it still seems difficult for us to talk about our locations inside several sets of social relations and practices where we are dominant rather than dominated. Unlike our subordinate position as women in relation to men, it seems as though our positions of power in relation to "other" women (and some men) do not need to be reflected upon. Indeed, it can be taken for granted and "left out" of feminist analyses. One problem with this is that what is "left out" often creeps back in again as the unstated, taken for granted and "normal" subject "Woman" in much feminist writing and politics (Kline 1989; Hull et. al. 1982; Simons 1979).

I do not mean that first person accounts must be included in everything that feminists write. In particular, I think that the confessional mode taken up by some white feminists talking about racism, for example, has limited and sometimes negative implications. Indeed, there are times when white women's guilt-ridden stories seem to be introduced in order for them to receive direction, praise or absolution from women of colour, as though such confessions were what is required. However real our feelings of guilt may be, to shift the discussion of racism in the university or the women's movement to white women's pain in dealing with our feelings, centres white women while marginalizing those who are subjected to racist practices (Spelman 1988). Focussing on individual feelings of guilt also tends to reduce questions of racism to matters of attitude, while ignoring social relations and practices of racism and how they might by taken up politically.

Thus accounts of "women's experience," including mine, cannot stand as unproblematic and unmediated truths about the category "Woman" or any actual woman's life. Such accounts do not and cannot constitute all there is to know about women's experience, even if we presumed that such complete knowledge were possible. Any account of experience, whether it be in the first, second or third person, is a mediation, an interpretation employing narrative strategies and forms of theory in its telling. Moreover, there are many and shifting truths about women's experience, although it's not at all arbitrary which of these truths comes to be seen as the truth that counts, including the truths that count as feminism. The kinds of personal and political stories of shifting locations which I have in mind are produced and lived through relations of power and difference (Corrigan 1990). It is here that Pratt's account and Mohanty's and Martin's interpretation of it are both evocative and provocative. They acknowledge many women's (and their own) desires for a stable and easily identifiable home or fixed truth within feminism. But they also confront the exclusions and oppressions which the satisfaction of that desire would entail in contemporary North America.

**The Second Story**

A white-skinned, middle class, heterosexual woman, who is also an immigrant to Canada, I entered graduate school in 1983 and soon felt "at home" in many ways. I encountered teachers and students who have had a profound impact on how I see the world and how I see myself. I have felt very privileged to be part of discussions which pushed and challenged the boundaries of academic disciplines, of marxism and of feminism in particular. I was privileged in a different sense as well; before returning to graduate school for an M.A. I had been able to save up enough money to pay fees and live for the first year without loans or part-time work. Then, and for each year until I finished my Ph.D, I received a scholarship, on which I could live in relative comfort. This enabled me to hang around and to attend all sorts of events and discussions outside of formal courses, to get involved in time-consuming student politics and to make studying a full-time endeavour for several years.

Speaking metaphorically there is a "division of labour" among graduate students, as there is in the university as a whole and in the capitalist social formation of which it is a part. Speaking of the graduate school I know best, students are divided in two main categories — those who study full-time and those who study part-time. Most classes are taught at night, drawing a mixture of full- and part-time students. The few day-time classes involve mostly full-time students who do not have conflicting working schedules, paid or un-paid. There is too a division in how courses are taken up and taught: night-courses are more oriented towards practice or service and day-time courses toward theory. The latter then become sort of advanced seminars where new topics and ideas are discussed. It was largely in these classes and during day-time seminars and meetings that I learned the language and ways of being a "serious graduate student." This was not a role that appeared ready-made to be picked up, nor was it one that I initially sought. In due course, however, I invested a lot of time and labour pursuing graduate studies. Obtaining scholarships provided one of the material conditions enabling me to spend a great deal of my time becoming competent for and in that position. As one of the very few students who did not hold down one or more part-time jobs to finance my schooling, and who did not parent children, I finished my dissertation relatively quickly and obtained a research fellowship and then a junior position in the department where I had studied.

So far I have talked mostly about material conditions such as scholarships and full-time studying. In spite of my comfort and "success" in these respects, I have often experienced life and work in academia as full of tensions, contradictions and seductions. These conflicts were not focussed on the everyday struggle to survive or to find enough time and energy to do the work required to get through graduate school. Before I decided to study full time I had worked as a community activist in Toronto for several years. This work was every bit as exhausting as that of a graduate student. Indeed, my initial decision to return to graduate school came out of "burn out" and frustration with community work as practiced in Toronto. As a community activist, I had tried, rather unsuccessfully, to make use of marxist theory. One of the frustrations I (and many others) encountered in graduate school was the tension involved in trying to think through quite abstract forms of knowledge in order to analyze my personal knowledge and experience as a community worker. Theories of the welfare state, for example, were not just read as conceptual arguments of intellectual debate but were constantly brought to bear on political situations and organizations that were familiar. Often the theories seemed to come up short, they started in the wrong end or they were not really about anything other than debates within a theoretical universe.

I was not initially drawn to do feminist work in university, but gradually I was attracted to feminist courses and the milieu around them. I attended seminars and lectures organized through the Women's Centre. Much of what feminist students and teachers were talking about made sense to me: I could recognize myself in what I was hearing and reading. We were invited to "speak from our own experience." Moreover, feminist (and marxist) writers and teachers offered ways of critiquing dominant relations of power and forms of knowledge. I felt that I was beginning to get a handle on some of the problems I had faced as a community worker. I found the interactions and arguments between marxism and feminism fascinating, especially the ways in which writers attempted to develop a political economy of women's oppression by integrating analyses of class and gender as social relations (Rubin 1975; Sargent 1981; Smith 1984). I later tried to deal with questions of gender and class relations in my thesis work.

Academic knowledge production, including feminist (and socialist) knowledge production, takes place in and through social relations of power and material conditions. As we make those social relations and material conditions the subject of feminist inquiry, it is important to reflect critically on how each of us came to be constituted and how we constitute ourselves as subjects and objects in relations we want to understand. It is in this context that I examine how I was able to do my work as a graduate student. Women going through ostensibly the same program are positioned and position themselves differently within it. The various experiences of the five women writing in this book are illustrations of that: We came to graduate school through diverse routes and have been working through it quite differently, with very different effects and memories. I can see now that one reason why I came to feel "at home" among academic feminists was that most of their talk, research and writing spoke to or about women like me.

### The Third Story

A few months ago I made a presentation for a seminar series at the university where I work. I talked about how I had eschewed any discussion about my own history when I wrote my Ph.D. thesis. It was only later that I began to acknowledge the strong connections between my life before and outside the university and the topics and debates that interested me as a graduate student. The particular link that I was trying to make in that seminar was between some archival material on visiting nurses in Toronto in the early twentieth century, and my childhood with parents who were doctor and nurse in a small, Norwegian town. It wasn't that I had been unaware of these connections before, I just didn't think it was "proper" to write them into my thesis. Although nobody was telling me this, doing so didn't seem right; it did not fit what I had been trained to think of as academic writing. Moreover, bringing in autobiographical stories seemed to raise more questions rather than answers, leaving uncertainties rather than conclusions.

After I finished my thesis, I wrote a paper about the work of visiting nurses for a conference on the history of education in Canada. I tried to grasp the social and historical specificity of nurses' practice, while at the same time placing their work in relation to class, gender, ethnicity and race and to state formation and nation-building in English Canada. I used the archival materials to argue that visiting nurses' practice, and especially their production of knowledge about "other" women and children, could be understood as Anglo-Saxon, middle class women organizing class and gender relations through the practices and discourses of (local) state formation. I pointed to conflicts, ruptures and difficulties in nurses' work, showing that several nurses resisted the demands made of them, refused to write up reports and to behave "properly." A few nurses took positions in defiance of physicians and nursing supervisors and got themselves fired. Concluding the paper I drew some tentative parallels between the observations and reports made by nurses in the early twentieth century Toronto and the work of feminist activists, researchers and theorists in the 1980s and 1990s. I did not feel that I was able to do this last part very well. I realized that I knew very little about the lives and histories of the women I was writing about.

Nevertheless, it was an adequate paper. A journal published it with some revisions (Dehli 1990). When I started to rewrite it, I began to do a very different reading of the paper and to rethink the data which had been its basis. I completed the rewriting, sent the paper off to the editors, but continued to think about visiting nurses and nurses' work. There were so many questions which I had not raised and so many connections which I had not made. Why? In writing it is impossible to say everything. You have to make choices among the points you want to make, the data you draw on and the interpretations you bring to bear. In preparing a paper for an academic conference and for a scholarly journal, I shaped my speaking and writing in a way that could be understood as "competent" within those settings. As I was thinking through how I had written that paper, I could see that the conventions which I followed made me exclude any reflections on myself as a subject in the text or in its making.

The superficial treatment of public health and school nurses in my thesis, and my retreat from important questions and connections in the subsequent paper were more than simply leaving out superfluous material. I was avoiding questions which felt too personal, too close to home. What I left out of the thesis and the paper, were the many links between early twentieth century nursing in Toronto, my childhood in Norway, as well as connections to the work I have been doing as a community worker and an academic since 1973. Although I had initially been moved by the nursing records because their accounts sounded so familiar, to write about these connections then seemed almost self-indulgent. I found it hard to think and write sociologically about myself. In the meantime, taking part in courses and seminars, as well as reading papers such as those by Pratt, Martin and Mohanty (among others), helped me to rethink my past and present in light of the new understandings they provided. There is a nurse in that history who has been and is very important to me and the work that I do.

### The Fourth Story
I grew up in a small town in Norway in a family of medical

professionals: my mother is a nurse, my father a doctor. They have run a family practice together for forty years in the house where my two older brothers, one older sister and I grew up. Two of my father's uncles were also doctors, as were three of his cousins. Later, my sister and one brother went to medical school and both of them are now family practitioners in the agricultural region where we grew up. My doctor-brother married a nurse and together they run a medical office very similar that of my parents. As children we heard a lot of talk about this work. Patients were coming and going in the house all the time. An important part of my identity as a child and teenager was as the "doctor's daughter."

My mother and I have had many conversations about her work and about her struggle to get into nursing school in the late 1930s. She was the youngest in a family of three daughters, and she was the only one to get any schooling beyond grade eight. Although they were not poor, her parents were not well off and there was no money for "extra" schooling. Her father did not think it necessary or suitable for their youngest daughter to train for an occupation other than marriage and motherhood. But she was determined, and saved up money by working for a couple of years as a domestic servant in Oslo and then as an aide in a home for the elderly. There was not much to save from, but somehow she managed to get into nursing school and to complete her training. After the war, she married her childhood sweetheart who was then a medical student. The two of them later set up a family practice in the small town where they were both raised.

When I was reading the records of public health and school nurses in Toronto I had an image of them being very much like my mother. From the personnel records, I could see that many of those nurses came from small towns and rural areas. Perhaps they too had had to struggle as my mother did to train for one of the very few professions open to women at that time? How did they see themselves in relation to the women and children who were their patients? How did they negotiate their relations with doctors and supervisors? What happened to them if or when they married and had children? Who among them chose to go into nursing as an alternative to marriage, as a way of working closely with women? Did the experiences of the few school and public health nurses in Toronto who were not Anglo-Saxons differ from those who were? As I was working through the rewriting of the paper I was remembering how much my mother's and father's work shaped our childhood. Because they worked together in the house where we also lived, there was a very visible continuity between the complex relations between nurse and doctor, wife and husband, father, mother and children. My parents worked hard in their professional practice and on top of that my mother, like most women, did all of the housework and childrearing. From her I learned to work hard and to discipline myself, to become a "good girl" and a "good student." Part of that learning was about managing desire, controlling pain and deferring pleasure — being patient until the work was done. By her example we learned to keep the peace, that you should not yell, shout and argue, that you didn't slam doors or call each other names.

Years later when we talk together my mother tells me of other layers of her experience, layers which I could not or would not see before. She talks about how tired and angry she often felt, how she struggled to get time for herself. Another story which is hard for me to hear is the relief she felt when I, the youngest, moved away from home. Slowly we begin to talk to each other about relationships with men, often indirectly by way of stories and experiences of others. Through all this I have to constantly rethink the ways in which I have framed the image of my mother as the heroic worker who is also the good mother and good wife (Trinh 1989; Steedman 1986).

And yet, it would be wrong to describe this family life as stifling, repressed and without pleasure. It would also be wrong to draw a picture of my mother as a submissive woman who quietly accepted prescribed feminine roles as nurse, wife and mother. Indeed, she challenged such prescribed expectations to become a nurse. Moreover, it would be a distortion to say that she was and is passive in all her relations with my father, her children or the community in which she lives. Through family and neighbourhood networks, particularly with other women, she is very active in several community organizations, especially ones involved in health care and services for the elderly. As a nurse and an activist in women's voluntary social service organizations, she has always worked with and for women. She does a lot of counselling and referrals for women and girls about sexuality, abortion and abuse, and she does this with a lot of caring, empathy and support in a small, conservative town where there is no hospital, no shelter, no feminist services of any kind, nor any place to go when a woman or child is raped, beaten and abused, or when a girl or woman needs an abortion. She's a firm believer in women's right to reproductive choice, although like many women of her generation (she's seventy) she has never labelled herself a feminist.

When I return to Norway for visits — which is not often since we live on two different continents — we talk about how the pretty and proper facades of heterosexual family life in that small town and rural region are not what they seem. Through her work she has gained insights into the lives and experiences of women in rural Norway which both unsettles notions of "home" as a place of comfort and harmony for women and notions of Norway's claim to being a country where women are well on their way towards equality with men. Standards of living for women in Norway are among the highest in the world and until recently there was nearly full employment. Health care services are free and accessible and women have right to abortion on demand. Many women are active and prominent in organized politics; in the current Labour government the Prime Minister is a woman, and the party claims to have a feminist agenda. I could go on with these general statements, however, these "facts" about Norway are ones I have learned to remember as ways to describe "where I am from." What I rarely tell are stories in which I am locating myself or people with whom I have lived, such as my mother.

As I write about this, it seems to me now that so much of my knowledge of the different experiences of women's oppression comes from my mother. Then why is it that I feel as though my childhood memories, the ways in which I have constructed them and the talks with my mother, are improper or inadequate bases for feminist academic knowledge which claims that the personal is political?

None of this knowledge entered my thesis or the paper I wrote about visiting nurses in Toronto. Although I know that my relation to my mother and to my father has a lot to do with why I was so intrigued by records of school and public health nurses' work, I could not write this into a thesis or an academic paper. Working through the academic exercise of writing a paper again, however, has made me rethink parts of my own history and how I have come to be in the locations where I am now, doing the work that I do. I also think about what I have been able to see and what I have avoided seeing in the memories and pictures I have of my own childhood, of my parents and of the community where I grew up. I remember my childhood as very happy and comfortable, yet I feel now that I have to confront some uncomfortable features of it. I ask myself how our comfort and happiness was predicated on not just the subordination of my mother to my father, but on other forms of subordination and exclusion as well. In our home there was no physical or psychological abuse that I can remember. My father assumed his dominant position in the family as a matter of course. He rarely asserted his power in explicit ways. The few occasions when he did stand out clearly in my mind because I was the target of his anger, refusing as a teenager to submit to his code of dress and sexual behaviour.

There were other unsettling features as well, such as the subtle boundaries that were drawn in a small town and rural area to separate "us" from "them." Some boundaries were clearly about class, others were drawn around those who "real-

ly belonged" in the district and those who were "newcomers."
My mother's kin, for example, have lived in this agricultural
area for as many generations as anyone can trace them, since
the 1490s! My father's belonging was somewhat more tenuous
(although never really questioned), as his paternal grandfather
had "only" arrived in the late nineteenth century as a school
principal. Since the early 1980s, "newcomers" to the area have
included a small number of non-Norwegian, non-white im-
migrants and refugees. In relation to them, boundaries are
drawn even more sharply, now with the added markers of race
and nationality. How do I, my parents and brothers and sisters
participate in those practices?

The maintenance of harmony and comfort of small town
and rural community life is part of women's work. Some of this
work involves formal and informal networks of assistance and
mutual aid. Another side of it, however, has to do with regulating behaviour and identity to a rather narrow range of implicit
and explicit norms. The effects are often cruel to those who are
in any way "different." Without any direct comment, we as
children knew who the kids were who represented "trouble,"
whose parents were poor, whose mothers were found lacking,
who came from "broken homes," whose fathers could be seen
drunk in the street. Some of these differences were clearly
markers of class, while others were experienced and negotiated
differently by girls/women and boys/men through the regulation of sexuality and gender relations. Like many other teenage
girls, I could hardly wait to move away from the claustrophobic
strictures of the town's surveillance and conformity. At eighteen
I moved to a different area of Norway and at twenty to Canada,
where I have lived and worked ever since. My ability to leave
was predicated on initial financial support from my middle
class parents and on access to a Canadian university.

As an immigrant from one of the Scandinavian countries
entering university, my experience of being an immigrant in
Canada has been quite different than what is often presumed
within the discourses on immigrant women. Indeed, it is quite

rare for me to be positioned as an immigrant woman by, for example, having to answer the question: "Where are you from?" or more consequentially for employment, "Do you have Canadian experience?" The practices of state agencies, employers and university admissions departments (to mention some) which tie together skin-colour and "accents" with being an immigrant, thus producing racist discrimination and exclusion for many, produce a kind of invisibility and erasure for me. In contrast to many immigrant women, these assumptions provide a whole range of advantages for me: I am included as a "Canadian" as a matter of course. My past elsewhere and my foreign identity are rarely taken up as problematic. On the few occasions when it becomes a matter of discussion, I am made to feel that being Scandinavian is wholly positive. On the other hand, I find that since I do not belong to any organized collectivity of Norwegians, and since my sameness is taken for granted, I rarely talk about the twenty years of my life before I moved to Canada. Coming here felt like starting a whole new history quite disconnected from that past.

The power of racism works to construct the category "immigrant woman" in ways which benefit me, which allow me to pass as a "Canadian." In the context of this paper, this means that I am rarely expected to account for my identity, or for my history of moving to this country, to explain where and what I was before I settled here. Writing about Toronto school nurses pushed me to begin to think about connections which I had not been able or willing to see before, especially between my work as a sociologist and feminist and my mother's work as a nurse.

## Conclusions

I have felt quite threatened at times when the relations and forms of knowledge in which I have become competent have been challenged. I have found it difficult to confront my own reactions and to move forward. But I also know that I have to do that confronting, and with it go through processes of change, because knowledge-production in universities is a terrain of conflict not just between women and men but among women. Our differences are not just discursive or theoretical; they are material, embodied and political, as we struggle against or conform to modes of knowing and being in the world, as we learn to channel our desires in socially prescribed ways, but also as we continue to interrupt, disrupt, subvert, as we fail, run away, get sick, feel stressed, have breakdowns. Even as I move between wanting to belong and have a home within academic feminism, the metaphor of the home conjures up conflicting images: promises of a harmonious and intimate safe place and at the same time the heavy price paid by girls and women in abuse, oppression, exclusion and regulation.

In order to overcome classist, racist and homophobic practices within universities and among feminists, women who find ourselves — by whatever route — on the dominant side of those relations cannot expect working class, non-white and lesbian women to do the critical work of pointing out what discrimination and oppression is or how it works. For example, racism and anti-semitism are social relations. White and non-Jewish women are part of those relations; they are embedded in the institutional practices in which we work. Racism and anti-semitism are not fixed or immutable but are socially organized within particular, historical relations and are therefore changeable. While listening to and reading what non-white and Jewish women are saying and writing is important, it is crucial for white feminists to examine how non-Jewish whiteness works to position us in relations of power over other women, for example within universities, and how we might change those relations.

If we who work as feminists inside academic institutions want to grasp our own complex positioning as subjects in relations of power and knowledge, it is necessary to locate our analysis on the terrain of practices and social relations of the academic work organization that we are part of. That is, we need to see both those relations in which *we* exercise power (powers of inclusion and exclusion, powers of naming what counts as feminist theory, for example), as well as those relations in which we are subordinated or excluded (by individual men or through institutional practices which undermine feminist research, teaching and writing).

In addition, we might do well to examine the different conditions which made it possible for us to study as well as to reflect on our investment in building a harmonious and secure "home" for ourselves in academic feminism. My early learning of self-regulation and discipline, of postponing pleasure "until the work was done" and of arguing by way of reasoning has been very conducive to the social relations and form of knowledge production that prevail in graduate school. The hidden curriculum of higher education rewards middle class students, thus producing and reproducing class relations. From an early age I learned to displace and express emotions, passions, joy, rage and conflict through reasoning, talk and distanced, third person accounts. (Who is that "third" person anyway?) Many writers, Valerie Walkerdine (1987) among them, describe procedures of transforming conflict into discourse as a key "normalizing" feature of bourgeois social regulation. Although appearing normal and natural, these processes of transformation are taught and learned — or not — in a complex web of social relations. Ironically, the process of becoming competent within the university and its forms of knowledge production seems to require not just a transformation, but a forgetting of emotion, desire, pain or pleasure, making it risky and difficult to take up the kinds of "personal" questions which we raise in this book.

In this paper I have begun to remember and to connect the work I do now with the locations and relations which I have lived and live. What I have hoped to do is to add to the discussion and to think about how white, middle class, heterosexual feminists working in academia can rethink the conditions of our being here and how we might resist the seductions of the university as a home. It seems to me that it is not only parts of our individual selves which are displaced and excluded through academic discourse and practice but all those selves which academics categorize as "other" — those who have not "mastered" the revered reasoning practices or who display "too much" feeling, desire or anger. Thus the struggles to unsettle the social relations of academic feminism are not just individual and personal, but collective and political.

## Endnotes

1. Although I take responsibility for errors and omissions, this paper has come out of a long, collective process. I received critical comments from Kate McKenna, Himani Bannerji, Linda Carty and Susan Heald as well as from Nancy Jackson, Linzi Manicom and Harry Smaller and participants in OISE's Critical Pedagogy/Cultural Studies seminar series.

# But Who Speaks for Us? Experience and Agency in Conventional Feminist Paradigms

*by Himani Bannerji*

. . . . . . . . . . . . . . . . . . . . . . . . . . .

## The Personal and the Political: Beginning from Our "Selves"

*One always learns better with blood.*

An old Columbian proverb

It has been difficult to write about being a student and a teacher in Canada. I would rather not have learnt or taught all the lessons that I did in these classrooms which mirror our everyday world. But there is no better point of entry into a critique or a reflection than one's own experience. It is not the end point, but the beginning of an exploration of the relationship between the personal and the social and therefore the political. And this connecting process, which is also a discovery, *is* the real pedagogic process, the "science" of social science.

First — there are colonial memories and memories of underdevelopment and neocolonialism. I grew up in Pakistan and India. Both countries were liberated through a long struggle for independence. The white man finally had left us, the states were ours, but inscriptions and fossils of colonialism lay everywhere, though often unrecognizable as such because they were so effectively internalized. I went to a "good" school, where everything was taught in English, and which served the children of the ruling class. Here Bengali, my mother tongue, the main language of nationalist culture of my region, with its hundreds of years of script and literature, was subordinated to Shakespeare. And later, sitting in the library of Presidency College under the portrait of Professor Richardson,[1] I did not know that I was a part of Macaulay's design for creating a special class.[2] Great literature or culture were universal, we learnt. They transcend space and history. English literature and language seemed ours by the same logic. They surpassed the little historical local England and embodied a state of cultural perfection. So we never quite thought that Charles Dickens, for example, had a particular local home and a daily social belonging.

My alienation from this "universal culture" began in England. That "our" Dickens might have looked at me in the streets of London, as others did, with a thinly veiled hostility — and not seen our common ground in the "universality of a refined literary sensibility" — became apparent to me many years ago in Porto Bello Road. In that poor district, lying in a damp room, reflecting on my days at art galleries, book stores and landmarks such as John Keats' house, I was faced with a reality for which I was unprepared. I felt small and bewildered, and put up a struggle to keep something of myself from vanishing and to maintain a little sense of significance. Though I did not know it then, I was being produced as "the other," as "different," but not neutrally different, not just as a cultural variation on the theme "human," but as "different and inferior." But at this time I only suffered from this at the level of feelings — feelings that had not yet been named, interpreted and become my experience. As yet I had no shared world or any social/political analysis, nor points of comparison. My alienation was produced everywhere — by everything — and it inverted itself to a thought of pure oneness with one's social environment, of belonging, to a longing for "home."

That great classroom of the Western world into which I was thrown head-first in England remains with me, as does the institutional classroom. When I came to study as a non-white "foreign student" in Canada — in streets, personal interactions, and in the classrooms and halls of the University of Toronto — my learning continued. I was a student in the English department, where my self and interests were rendered more silent than I would have thought possible. I remember feeling confused and a growing sense of frustration and rage. Nothing that was relevant to me seemed to count. I realized the degree to which I was a marginal member of the discipline, whose "universality" by this time had given way in my mind to being highly local and particular, whose historicity and ideological character became daily more visible. Deprived of a general sense of social belonging, of being a comfortable user of the local cultural grammar, divided by my gender, race and marxism, I was an "outsider" in and to my discipline and the classrooms that I inhabited. Often I was the only non-white student in these classes. Other students would talk among themselves with ease and were willingly responded to by the professors even when there were disagreements. I looked for reasons for their sense of a shared reality. It was not in their reading or thinking ability — because I had both — but in their "whiteness" together (middle class Anglo/European cultural heritage and white skin) and their political commonality. They carried on discussions as though I was not there, or if I made a comment which introjected my anti-colonial marxist view of English literature into the discourse or compared it to "other" literatures (third world or "black" literature), the flow would be interrupted. Then they would look at each other and teachers would wait in the distance for me to finish. There might have been some uneasy and unclear response at times — but generally no one would pick up my points. I would feel out of place, my face warm, and wished I had not spoken. Mercifully the conversation would resume and the waters close above my head. I was an outsider and not much by the way of intellectual performance was expected of me. In fact no one thought of me — for or against — in any real way. I repeated my M.A., kept very good grades, took my comprehensives and sometimes got asked by eminent English professors whether I felt cold in *saris*, ate beef or was comfortable in English. Wading through trivia, fluent in English, but not in aestheticized colonialese, I searched for ways to understand what was happening to me and whether and how it also happened to others. In this way I wanted to create my own experience by understanding in social and political terms these events and interactions which frustrated and thwarted me. To make a long story short — I found Frantz Fanon, George Jackson, Angela Davis and the Black Panthers, Karl Marx, Che Guevara and African liberation movements, Vietnam. And redeemed academia by discovering Raymond Williams, C.B. McPherson, Frederic Jameson, and finally and irrevocably found feminist literature. By the time I discovered them all I had become rather useless to English, and English to me, as practiced by the University of Toronto, the Harvard of the North. Having explained at length the title of my doctoral dissertation — "Conservative Ideology and the Educational Ideas of S.T. Coleridge" — making a distinction for my teachers between "thought" and "ideology" — I finally left the department with a half-finished thesis. As a marxist and a feminist, conscious of racism and imperialism, I dropped out of the department as does a leaf from a branch when its stem has dried. Upon leaving the classroom I experienced relief. Now there was the crude harassment of everyday life, sexist racism[3] but not the subtle, refined cruelty of intellectual racism and colonialism.

I concentrated on writing poetry, political-cultural criticism and on articulating myself somehow to the women's movement that existed in Toronto. But there, in the place I least expected, a naive believer at this point in "sisterhood is powerful," eager to add my voice, to speak from my own experience as an active participant in the revolution of half of the world's population, I experienced my deepest disappointment. With a change of rhetoric, my English classroom was there all over again, in fact the dramatis personae often overlapped. Once when young I was let down by my bourgeois belief in the universality of "culture." In my mid-thirties I went through a similar but worse experience. I realized painfully, to paraphrase Orwell, that "all are women, but some are more women than others." Controversies over International Women's Day, which I celebrated with fervour, conveyed to me the astounding revelation that imperialism was not a "women's issue." Readings informed me that class and gender struggles were to be separately conceived and waged, that women were "class-less," a "caste" perhaps, and patriarchy was an "autonomous" power system. And a growing essentialism as well as a perverse biologism persisted through all this. Racism was not even mentioned as a real issue by the "Canadian women's movement."[4] Our lives, our labour remained unmentioned, and intellectual/cultural production unsolicited, in the annals of publications of the (Canadian) Women's Press. We were at best a separate category of sub-women — "immigrant," "visible minority," "ethnic," "black," later "women of colour." All were labels — except "black" — with no political history of militancy behind them. Here in relation to feminism and the women's movement my otheriza-tion was even more overtly accomplished than in the university — and in the context of an assumed "sisterhood," the damage was much deeper. The greatest gain however, was meeting with young black women, whose experience and politics matched with mine, whose poetry along with mine named our world. Affirmed by them in a fundamental way in my reality, I felt the legitimacy of my anger as a "black" woman. In those days we thought that whoever was "not white" in a racist society was a part of the great political metaphor — "black." The British use of this term in *Race and Class*, for example, or in anti-racist organizing, legitimized our choice of political self-description. We had not yet become ethnically or culturally territorial about our political identities.

And — resenting entrepreneurialism, lacking a space for developed intellectual work and with a smouldering anger about being indirectly "pushed out" — I returned to school. This time in sociology, at OISE — where the feminist marxism of Dorothy Smith, the generally more permissive attitude towards political intellectual work and that I was working on my three interests — India, communism and political theatre — mitigated to some extent the institutional and social forms of alienation, namely racism, otherization and "feminist" aggression in the monopoly of definition of the term carried out by white Anglo/European women.

All this while, however, like Shente of Brecht's *Good Person of Setzuan*, I wore another hat as another persona. From 1970 to 1974, I was teaching at Victoria College as a part-time lecturer in the English department and from 1974 to 1989 I was a temporary, contractual, part-time, piece-work teacher of part-time students at Atkinson College, York University. In the last year I have, at this late stage of my life, finally found favour in the eye of the establishment and become an assistant, non-tenured (but possible) professor. Once, a long time ago, I was a tenured faculty in India — from 1965 to 1969. I came to Canada on leave from my job — and it took twenty years to find myself comparable employment.

But as a teacher in social science and sociology my difficulties are of equal magnitude — and of the same kind — as those experienced as a student of English. Of the many problematic aspects of my teaching relations I will speak of a few key ones — and conceptualize them in terms of who I am and who the students are, what I teach and how.

Once again I must begin from myself. From my body as a political signifier. The gendered perception of my sex receives a further negative (and also a latently violent) reference from a prevailing racist common sense. This perception of the students is not neutral — it calls for responses from them and even decisions. I am an exception in the universities, not the rule. As a body type I am meant for another kind of work — but nonetheless I am in the classroom. And what is more, I am authority. I grade and therefore am a gatekeeper of an institution which only marginally tolerates people like us in scarcity rather than in plenty. What I speak, even when not addressing gender, race and class, does not easily produce suspension of disbelief. Working in a course on "Male-Female Relations" which I co-designed and co-taught for six years with a colleague — who is male, white, older, taller, bigger, and a full-time faculty — I saw the specificity of student response towards me, where I had continuously to work against my subordination. Whenever expertise or administration was at issue, my status as an equal worker had to be forcefully underlined. It was rarely, except technically, seen as my course as well. The overall attitude of the students towards me in this course was not exceptional. It fits with other courses which I taught or teach by myself. It is not surprising that this combination of racist social practices, media presentations and cultural common sense all made it initially hard for us to settle into a stable professor-student relationship.

I have written elsewhere about this experience of teaching.[5] Suffice it here to say that there were also "other" students, as I was the "other" teacher, and together we found that neither sociology (not even the conventional marxist variety) nor feminism (not even marxist feminism) spoke to our lives, our experiences, histories and knowledges of the world. The existing literature, the conventional paradigms — of both left and "bourgeois" sociology/feminism, or radical ones — had little or tangential application for us. Neither in the sociology of the family as presented by Eli Zaretsky (male marxist), nor in the political economy of the marxist/socialist feminists, nor in the books on "our repression/oppression" in terms of sexuality, did we find much that spoke of our lives — either as lived by us in the West or in those parts of the world homogenized from a metropolitan perspective as "the third world." Racism was and is considered a separate problem from sexism, and seen as a "black" problem. Making themselves "white" by the same stroke of the pen which gave and gives us this special/peculiar status — these women construct(ed) their separate world, which purportedly did not come into being through the same social relations that ours did. The absence, the gap, the silence regarding the presence of "others" or "their issues," did not bother the theoretical and investigative minds of these white feminists of all varieties. This physical non-representation in spacial/textual politics was not problematized. It was not remarked that non-white women were and are not seen as a real part of "feminist" textual production. The fact that this "exclusion" is organized by the very same principles that generate "inclusion" for white women still remains invisible to white feminists by and large.

Unvalidated in our bodies, experiences and theorization, we daily learnt and taught a literature, theoretical paradigms and methods that alienated us from our lives. Thus we were and are offered the possibility of a political or an intellectual agency on grounds and terms that are inauthentic to our lives and not created by us. This was and is quintessential alienation. The more we participate(d) in these processes, the more a giant edifice of knowledge augments the power of others over and against us. Where are we to turn? Where can we find interpretive frameworks and methods that are more than "alternative" and would go beyond "inclusion"? How can we gain an insight into the social relations and culture of advanced capitalism which allows for direct representation and a revolutionary political agency?

### Beginning from the "Other" End: A Critique of "Otherizing" Social Relations and Intellectual Modes

*Have you read the grievances some of our sisters express on being among the few women chosen for a "Special Third World Women's Issue" or on being the only Third World woman at readings, workshops, and meetings? It is as if everywhere we go, we become Someone's private zoo.*

Trinh T. Minh-ha
*Woman, Native, Other*

So far then, we get a glimpse of how it is that what Foucault called "knowledge/power" relations are inscribed all over my academic experience. It is obvious that the production of knowledge is a part of social production as a whole, and as much attention must be paid to the social relations of "knowledge" as to its content. Teacher-student relations in the classroom, relations among the students themselves, and the world outside the class which we enter in the pursuit of "objective," "positive" knowledge, all influence the form and content of our learning. All social and cultural relations and forms, both of oppression and privilege, directly and indirectly shape what and how we learn, or even whether — as exemplified by my "drop-out" behaviour — we wish to continue "learning" at all. Even if we can no longer speak in such quaint nineteenth century ways as "education educes the whole soul of man" (sic), we do know that knowledge comes in two types — a producer's knowledge and a consumer's knowledge. In the former we participate in our learning as creators and in the latter as mere functionaries and hoarders of information or "facts." The overall social relations that construct(ed) my classrooms demonstrate the disincentives to learning and teaching as non-white women.

If the social relations of production of knowledge in institutional settings constitute a silent but powerful set of learning imperatives, the content itself — texts, literature, analytic/interpretive frameworks, methods or paradigms (in short what we call curriculum) — presents us with the other half of our problem. They not only teach "facts" or supply "information," but actually create what John Berger calls "ways of seeing": perspectives and interpretive modes which encompass systematic ideological stances, but also go beyond them in forming an overall cultural social vision and praxis.[6] This textual mediation also does not inhabit a separate social sphere. It actually draws on and systematizes, and often uncritically, cultural common sense and everyday practices and invests them with the status of knowledge (as social facts, norms, etc.) as well as knowledge-creating procedures (theories and methods). These textual omissions and commissions confer a normalcy to reificatory textual devices and can, for example, naturalize orientalism and sexist racism. When practiced by ourselves they develop into grotesque forms of self-alienation. Sometimes an even more unusual situation results. A text which is coherent with my experience as a non-white woman, for example, when inserted into the tentacles of an alienating interpretive device, loses its original reference points and meaning, and becomes inert and inverted. Thus, *The Wretched of the Earth* in the light of O. Manoni's *Prospero and Caliban* becomes an example of Oedipal counterphobia of the colonized, or Angela Davis' *Women, Race and Class* an example of "black feminism," no more than just a "different" perspective in feminism.

These problems of generating the content or the curriculum point to fundamental aspects of knowledge production that affect us all positively or adversely. If the purpose of learning/teaching determines the type of knowledge produced, implicit in this knowledge is always a notion of political agency. The agency, whether it is active or passive, of a producer or of a consumer, varies according to the goal — which may either be social change or the continuation of the status quo. If knowledge is to be "active," that is, oriented to radical social change, then it must be a critical practice of direct producers, whose lives and experiences must be the basis for their own knowledge-making endeavour. What Paolo Freire called the "banking method" — treating the student as a storehouse of "facts" of a fixed content — is then out of the question.[7] This critical/active knowledge then is a basic form and part of a general political process — which relies on the subjectivity of the student and the teacher — and consciousness (both its products and forms) is seen as socially grounded.

The educational process consists of establishing transformative connections between how people live or act and how they think. The usefulness of this knowledge lies in its ability to give a reliable understanding of the world and to impact or change lives rather than simply to "function efficiently." Thus an "active" education begins from experience (the immediate and the local) through an understanding of the increasingly complex mediations which structure it and culminates into political effectiveness. The intellectual project of feminism is par excellence one example of such "active" knowledge.

Feminism ideally rests on a transformative cognitive approach, which validates subjectivity and direct agency.[8] It is disinterested in "expertise," which reduces women to outsiders and operators of the machinery of the status quo knowledge. Thus beginning from ourselves, with a project of self and social transformation (encoded in the slogan "the personal is political"), does not require an apology but, on the contrary, becomes a basic imperative. If this is the fundamental stance of feminist politics and pedagogy, then we are left with a puzzling situation for non-white women. What, we must ask, accounts for the reificatory or exclusionary textual and social practices which we, non-white women, encounter even in the context of feminist pedagogy? By what magic do we become textually invisible, or at best segregated into our special status, denied real agency and our lives constructed as peripheral to the everyday workings of society?

The answers to these questions do not lie in individual ill-will and racist conspiracies (though they may exist) but rather in the theories, methods and epistemologies used by feminists, and the cultural common sense within which they arise. In this feminist theory is no different from any other theory which serves different class and ideological interests (even when it does so unself-consciously — in the name of "women").

My project is to consider the basic epistemological standpoints of some of the major feminist approaches, ignoring their apparent political differences and labels. The organizing concepts for this assessment are central to any study of epistemology. They are generally presented in a binary relationship to each other and arranged in the following pair patterns:

general/universal and particular, essential/abstract and concrete, local/immediate and extralocal/mediated, part and
whole, experience/ consciousness and the mode of production,
and finally subjectivity and material conditions. As we might
notice, some of these pairs express the same content as the
others. The efficacy of any social theory is determined by its
ability to demonstrate and theorize adequately the formational
(i.e., non-oppositional) interplay between these different moments of social cognition. The explanatory, analytical and
descriptive/ethnographic task of social theory requires that it
be able to dis-cover the mediations[9] of different social moments
in non-polar terms, and bring out the "specificity" of any
fragment of experience by providing it with a general name as
well as with a particular authenticity at the same time. That is,
it must show how any situation/experience is distinctively,
particularly, locally itself and yet/also constituted by and ex-
emplary of social forces which lie in, around and beyond it. The
most "trivial" incident, understood in this way, can reveal
certain basic and necessary relations intrinsic to the social organization and forms of consciousness as a whole. At its best it
is a relational and an integrative analysis which needs a
deconstructive method to display the process of mediation. It
can both take apart and put back together (in a non-aggregative
fashion) an event or an experience within a wider context by
using a materialist theory of consciousness, culture and politics.
I characterize different feminist theories according to their
ability to comprehend and represent conceptually a mediational and formational view of social practice. Their ability to
accomplish a less one-sided social analysis and interpretation,
I claim, depends on their understanding and handling of
mediation.

Of the available feminist frameworks, I will begin with the
one which is most common — and which we learnt as our first
feminism. For this we have to turn to the type of
sex/gender/power relation in the works of Kate Millet, Betty
Friedan or Germaine Greer, for example, and their essentialist

interpretation of an earlier anthropological concept of patriarchy.[10] Patriarchy was denuded of its content as a general social organization and division of labour (for example, of hierarchical kinship relations among men or between elder female kin and younger male kin) or as an overall organization of the mode of production (a regulator of production, consumption, distribution and exchange). The concept of "patriarchy," (originally meant for the study of pre-capitalist social formations) was read as an unmediated form of power relations between men and women. The feminist interpretation of patriarchy distilled from it a universal theory of power — direct, interpersonal domination by (any) man over (any) woman.[11] Male need and power to dominate was seen as both intrinsic and original (biological/quintessential), and as socially manifested through "gender" relations. Patriarchy was found in its purest form (as original impulse or even instinct) in the domination of women in the area of sexuality, and relatedly in maternity. All other social relations and contradictions manifest this domination and are subsumed in the primary antagonism expressed in male-female gender relations. Man and woman face each other in opposition — their subjectivities in "essential" otherness and confrontation. This antagonistic otherness originates outside of history and social organization but provides their foundational ground.[12] The authentic ground of woman's subjectivity is presumed to rest on her unitary woman-self and otherness to man (two single and singular subjects with ontologically antithetical consciousnesses), assuming a global sameness for all women, trans-historically and socially, as well as trans-personally.

Feminist theory of this kind exposes, challenges and subverts its own version of patriarchy. This it does by positing a synthetic category called "woman" as a unified consciousness and a universal subject. The category is still based on otherness to man, but this otherness when undominated exists freely for itself as subject in the world. Feminist essentialism, with its hypothetical/synthetic woman subject, can not situate women in history and society. As such, it eradicates real contradictions among women themselves and creates a myth ("woman") and an abstraction, by isolating gender from all other social relations. This transcendence from history and from actual lives of people as inessential or accidental is entirely based on an idealist epistemology.

Gender and patriarchy, seen thus, become ideological constructs and lose their power as concepts for social analysis and, even as constructs, they are fundamentally paradoxical. The theorization rests on the assumption that what is "real" or universal is "essential" (supra-social/historical), while, at the same time deducing this "essence" and universality from historical and social particularities. The complex and constitutive mediation of an entire social organization is thus "ruptured" by disarticulating one relation — "gender" — and conferring on it an autonomous status and transcendent universality. This paradoxical theory is made credible less by any essential truth about women that it reveals than by relying on details of relations of power which are pervasively present in most societies we know about. Social history is thus portrayed as an endless repetition of an interpersonal patriarchal drama with a constant ratio of power and powerlessness held by the two protagonists.

Decontexting "patriarchy" or gender from history and social organization — which is structured by both cooperative and antagonistic social relations — obscures the real ways in which power works. Using this framework, we can not conceptualize a reality in which women are complicit and "gender" is implicated in, both creating and maintaining class and racist domination. Nor can we see the cooperative en-gendering of the social space of classes, or the simultaneity of this cooperation with the necessary subordination of women within the dominant and subordinate classes. Through this theorization we can not speak of women's experiences in relation to class and race (in the West). This pre-interpretation of reality valorizes all women *as woman* and at the same time denies their actual lived relations. That "race" (as a category for organizing ruling relations) or class become invisible in this essentialism is only logical.

This invisibility adds to the status quo of oppression. Working class white and non-white women do not have reasons to feel "equal" to the essentialist theorists. They are drowned rather than empowered by this generality. All notions of "sisterhood" break down in front of actual experience which resists this false universality according to which *all women* have identical subjectivities and are equally oppressed and certainly not by each other.[13] Feminist essentialism, in the end, becomes a cloak for smuggling in the interests of privileged women. As Elizabeth Spelman puts it, "'Woman' as an essentialist/universal category is a 'Trojan horse,'" (and) "the more universal the claim, the more likely (it is) to be false.... feminist theory provides a friendly home for white middle class privilege and concerns."[14]

Many white feminist theorists in recent years have become aware of the pitfalls of essentialism. Interest in the essential "other" of man (and its negation) has shifted to "other women."[15] Not entirely a spontaneous gesture of reflexivity, this is also a response to the vigourous dissatisfaction and anger of non-white women[16] and white and non-white lesbians. In the new theorization, experience, subjectivity and political agency have been at the centre of the debate. Here the particularity and immediacy of experiences of oppression by different groups of women have been theorized and politicized under the concept of "difference." Emphasizing diversity, particularity, multiple and changing subject positions and self-representation, the politics of difference has rejected the universalist position.

The admission of "experience" to theory has moved feminist theory into speaking of the concrete and the tangible. In Britain and the U.S., for example, it has been most forcefully brought to attention that racism is a central determinant of women's experience in advanced capitalism, as are, relatedly, poverty, discrimination and dispossession.[17] As non-white women have spoken up for themselves, so they have been valorized as "different" and granted, in theory, the right to equal access to a representational voice. A large section of the feminist mainstream accepts that only we can speak for ourselves, and that women's varied experiences provide the ground for multiple types of politics.[18]

This politics of "difference" is, however, not as unmixed a blessing as it appears to be. If the paradigm of feminist essentialism played up the general/universal at the cost of the sociocultural and historical particulars, this politics of difference errs on the side of the particulars, often making it impossible to see the forest for the trees. It invents multiple political personalities within one subject and invests expressions of these and other different subject positions with an equal and real value. This creates the possibility of a positive coexistence among them, without any regard for either experiential coherence or the genuinely antagonistic social relations that underlie the speech act or expression and thus provide the context of and the reasons for the "difference." This emphasis on experience and expression as the main form of political activity equates politics primarily with free speech/cultural expression within a general format of civil liberties. Often in the feminist context it means that so long as a white woman (middle class) does not speak for me, but gives me equal time (since she controls the space prior to my arrival), all is well. But being "equal" to white women who themselves are unequal on class and other grounds does not reflect on or bring into question the societies of fundamental inequality in which we live. Through this framework we can't "see" the overall social relations and common sense which organize the sexist racist experiences of nonwhite women, making their colour a socio-cultural signifier of a deeper and exploitative "difference." Furthermore, while concentrating mainly on the expression of our own oppression, it becomes difficult to keep other oppressions in sight, or to think beyond our own advancement. The task of overall change, that of re-organizing social relations of inequality as a whole, becomes peripheral to the main project.

The concept of "difference," therefore, clearly needs to be problematized. Where does such "difference" reside? Who are we "different" from? Upon reflection it becomes clear that the "difference" which is politically significant is not a benign cultural form. The "difference" which is making us "different" is not something inherent or intrinsic to us but is constructed on the basis of our divergence from the norm. Since non-white women vary enormously from each other, as do different groups of whites from each other and from us, it remains a question as to why white middle class heterosexual feminists do not need to use the "difference" argument for their own theory or politics? When questioned thus, "difference" becomes a matter of our *similarity* to each other as non-white women in a racist social organization which "otherizes" us, ascribing a self-ness/sovereignty to white women. It is only these racist modes which create political signifiers out of our skin colour, physiognomy, culture, etc., and produce oppressive experiences. Our "difference" then is not simply a matter of "diversities," which are being suppressed arbitrarily, but a way of noting and muting at the same time fundamental social contradictions and antagonisms. The concept of "difference," with its emphasis on expression/textual/linguistic view of social reality, obscures these antagonisms at the level of everyday life and overall (national or international) social and economic organization.[19] It prevents us from seeing that racism is not solely a "cultural"/ideological problem and that the ground of our racist oppression is the same as the ground of white privilege. In the name of "difference" we tend not to go beyond a rich and direct description of personal experience to a social analysis which will reveal the sameness of social relations that constructs the experience of "white" privilege and "black" oppression.

The politics of "difference" hides in its radical posture a neo-liberal pluralist stance, even when power and brutality are stressed as "differential" factors. Generally it amounts to advancing a metatheory of competing interests built on the concept of a free market. The political sphere is modelled on the market place and freedom amounts to the liberty of all political vendors to display their goods equally in a competition. But this view of society as an aggregate of competing individuals, or at best as fragmented groups or communities, makes the notion of an overall social organization theoretically inconceivable and thus unnameable. All such attempts are dismissed as totalizing and detrimental to individuality, uniqueness of experience and expression. Concepts such as capital, class, imperialism, etc., are thus considered as totalizing, abstract "master narratives," and untenable bases for political subjectivity since they are arrived at rationally and analytically, moving beyond the concreteness of immediate experience. And the master narrative of "patriarchy" (which the "difference/diversity" feminists do conform to — since they identify themselves as "feminists"), fractured through experience and locked into identity circles, also can not offer a general basis for common action for social change, without sinking into a fear of "essentialism" or "totalization."

Obviously a situation of equal representation is better than that of monopoly. And speaking in their own voice does "empower" people. Failing all else, even the speech act itself can become libratory. If the classrooms I inhabit(ed) had a discourse of "difference," we would not be so frustrated, outraged or silent. We would be the direct producers within the discourse. But what would we speak about? How would we communicate our particular ways of being and seeing to others who do not share our experiences? And what finally would be the objective of our speaking?

The refined particularism and individualism of the politics of "difference" not only avoids naming and mapping out the general organization of social relations, it also reduces the concept of experience from an interpreted, dynamic process of subjective appropriation of the social into a far more static notion of "identity." De-emphasizing the social and the historical in the interest of individual uniqueness, expanding at most as similarity of detail, the concept focuses on a content rather than a process and creates knowledge enclosures. Thus the stories we tell from our immediate life become the end of our political destination, rather than serving as the first steps to an active/interpretive definition of self, which bears a constitutive relation to our social world. That subjectivity arises in a shared "social" and mental space is obscured.

That this social space is riven with genuine antagonisms and contradictions, where the privilege of some women directly militates against the rights of many others, does not however prevent it from being "shared." It is a common social terrain inhabited by all. Occupying different parts of the social topography and allowing for differential access to social, economic and cultural resources and political power, does not exempt anyone from the possibility or the responsibility of naming what constitutes the social whole. Beginning and ending in "difference," i.e., a fragmented presentation of subjectivity, merely hinders us from facing/uttering the fact that a whole social organization is needed to create each unique experience, and what constitutes someone's power is precisely another's powerlessness. A rich description of an immediate experience is an indispensable point of beginning, but it must expand into a complex analysis of forms of social mediation.

The concept of "difference" opens and closes simultaneously some very basic epistemological and social questions. Opening the door to many experiences and possibilities, it closes out, in its fear of generalization and equation of subjectivity with immediate feelings and experience, any "social" explanation for these very same things. If it establishes anything larger and in common, it is by the simple principle of matching of detail. With each change in the configuration of details reality itself differs or changes. This empiricism equates each decontexted variation of detail — what immediately seems to be — with what actually happens. It is this empiricism which makes "difference" theories unusable beyond a politically or a discursively expressive gesture. At its widest, it expands into "issues" and "communities" which remain as discrete, self-enclosed ontological entities (with equal rights, however). Lacking an analysis of forms of consciousness and social relations, theories of "difference" lack the potential for a revolūtionary politics. Colonialism, imperialism, class or "race" — all concepts which require a broad historical and social scope — exist primarily as discursive practices, defying any systematic existence or naming outside of the individual's interaction with them. In the end they are converted into metaphors of "power" whose sources and reasons for continuation remain undefinable.

Even this best aspect of the liberal tradition can not provide a social analysis which uncovers or explains how it is that white and black women (in a racist society) arrive at opposite results/effects by sharing the same social relations.

And for that social analysis I turned to "marxist/socialist feminism," considering it a doubly revolutionary social project involving class and gender/patriarchy. But here the situation is even more complicated, in so far as representation/direct agency as well as issues of "race" are not the focus or basis of this social analysis. "Racism" and "race," as well as non-white women as producers of theory or politics, are generally absent from the textual world of "marxist/socialist feminism."[20] This absence is not only a matter of disappointment and acrimony for non-white women, but even more fundamentally it throws the whole theoretical and political project of marxist feminism into question.

If we assess marxist/socialist feminism in terms of its theory of agency and representation, we find little interest in either. We are clearly pitted in the midst of an unresolved relationship between two social projects premised on different grounds. The "marxism" or class analysis of marxist feminism is mainly a certain version of Marx's idea of "political economy." Sharing with their male counterparts the agenda of a "scientific" social analysis, feminist political economy is largely an attempt to situate women and the sexual division of labour in capitalist production. Feminists also equate marxism mainly with political economy and use the same positivist method for reading *Capital*, though in retaliation against the sexism and gender-blindness of male practitioners. The major marxist feminist achievement consists of annexing the home to capital, as a site for and function of, its reproduction.[21] That is, it makes public and economic the "private" form of capital-labour relations, as though by stripping it bare to its true economic functions. This economistic and productionist emphasis continues right through feminist political economy. The absence of women is rectified, and as the domestic labour and "wages for housework" debates indicate, women can now be seen as fully contributory to capital, producing "value" at home, "reproducing" to augment surplus value indirectly. In this attempt to make "the private" public, lived social relations and forms of consciousness that constitute a personal, cultural, home life — all dubbed "subjective" and therefore phenomenal — remain outside of the purview of an analysis of "class" and capitalism. An abstract and economistic reading of *Capital*, which ignores use value and the social and reduces the whole mode of production into "economy" (i.e., solely a sphere of exchange value and circulation), disattends Marx's analysis of capital as a *social relation* rather than a "thing." It is not surprising, therefore, that this economistic reading of *Capital* did not lead to a general appreciation of seemingly ideological-cultural factors such as "race" and ethnicity. That racism and sexism are necessary social relations for the organization of colonial or modern imperialist capitalism in the West seems to figure as an afterthought in recent writings.

But even as an "economistic" understanding of our world, feminist political economy needs to extend itself beyond its present state. In the Canadian case we need work that gives us a world of commodity production with producers as living, conscious agents rather than as functional assumptions of the production process, and that also presents the Canadian economy in its organizational and structural complexity. When delinked from its history as a white settler colony and its present as an imperialist capitalist state which continues to import labour on the basis of ethnicity, race and class — creating "class" in its own terrain — the Canadian economy becomes an abstraction. The erasure of the factors of "race," racism and continual immigration prevents an adequate understanding of the Canadian economy. The construction of the Canadian labour market (its segmentation) and capital accumulation in relation to uneven development or concrete forms of the exploitation of surplus value are important examples. Yet we know that an accurate economic characterization of the political economies of Britain, Canada and the U.S., for example, or of France and West Germany, can not be made without showing how fundamental a role "ethnicity" and "race" have played as organizational and administrative categories of both the economy and the state. The consciousness which marxist feminists acquired of "gender" and of women's contributory role in capital did not open their eyes to the social specificity of differential exploitation that actually exists in an economic organization.[22] Not even *functionally* did they apply the categories of "race" and ethnicity and attend to practices of racism to augment their understanding of capital. Only very recently, as a result of protest and analysis by non-white women themselves, do we hear the litany of "gender, race and class" recited in the introductions to essays/books on political economy.[23] But why is racism still at the level of being named rather than an integral part of the economic analysis?

The source of this failure in the political economy of marxist feminists lies in the abstraction characterizing their original positivist reading of marxism. This was further modernized with a sophisticated reading of capital and its state and ideology under the influence of Louis Althusser. As an antidote to the earlier positivist "economism" we received new theories of self-contained and self-reproducing but interlocking "structures" of society (determined by the economy in the *last* rather than the *first* instance), at which we arrived "scientifically" (ascending the steps of "generalities"). Experience, the self, the social and the cultural, that is, anything subjective, was abandoned as an ideologically contaminated form of unreality. The subjective dimension of class and class struggle, involving theorization of political agency and direct representation, became redundant to the consideration of revolution. In the name of "scientific" analysis, all bases for political subjectivities were erased and with them the complexities of different kinds of social contradictions.

The social space was then conceived as a chain of linked "structures" which somehow "reproduced" themselves and spun off into others by using human agents to fulfill their will and purpose.[24] The revolutionary thrust of Marx's writing on self-emancipation and the making of history, the relationship between politics and class consciousness, were irrelevant to the project. The subjective dimension of the revolutionary project was dismissed as "humanist" and "idealist," belonging to the pre-scientific revolution stage ("epistemological break") in Marx's development. Marxists with theories of political subjectivity involving experience and agency, such as Sartre, for example, theorists of different liberation movements, such as Fanon, or marxist writers of cultural and historical theories, such as Williams or Thompson, were hardly drawn upon (Sheila Rowbotham and a few others remain exceptional). Not only for non-white women alone, but for anyone interested in creating a revolutionary social movement at all, there is no *active*, conscious and creative, no fully subjective ground for direct political agency within the framework of Althusserian marxism. And since "racism" in these terms is considered a cultural/ideological — a superstructural — phenomenon. It can thus be dismissed, or relegated the status of a superficial attitudinal problem.

This objective, structural abstraction in the political economy of socialist/marxist feminists — which provides the theoretical groundwork for their overall social project — sits very uneasily with the utterly subjective position that they advance as "feminists" in their gender revolution. Marxist feminists themselves have commented at length on this dilemma, and phrased it in terms of an "unhappy marriage between marxism and feminism."[25] Latterly, "socialist feminists" have sought to question further as well as seek to reconcile this unhappy union. But they seem to have shunted aside an indepth consideration of the dilemma and decided that quantity can change quality even when the epistemological and analytical premises are antithetical. That is, they have added to the economic structural analysis another set of structures immediately out of the range of wage labour. The "private" realm of the family as a "social structure" and the "ideological structure" of patriarchy were added onto each other in the realms of public and domestic production. This economistic analysis has been supplemented by its counterpart in the radical feminist analysis of the "personal sphere," but without an effective integration in marxist theory. Topics such as motherhood and sexuality, picked up from radical feminism, have been included in texts on women's oppression as indicators of this merger, but have either been economistically interpreted or have found their place, though subordinate, alongside economic factors as "cultural/personal" aspects of the mode of production.

This "unhappy marriage of marxism and feminism" can not be dealt with, as Heidi Hartman has noticed, through either a subsumption of feminism in marxism[26] or through an arithmetical exercise which constructs a social whole by adding together qualitatively different epistemological stances. As Marx pointed out in the first thesis on Feuerbach, an objectivist ("materialist") standpoint is fundamentally opposed to a subjectivist ("idealist") one, and both stand in equal antithesis to a reflexive, historical materialist standpoint which conceives of the social in terms of "sensuous, practical human activity."[27] Lacking a concept of a cultural social formation and narrowing the social to mean the economic, marxist feminists create an unbridgeable gap between self, culture and experience, and the world in which they arise and have little to say about political subjectivity.

No real and coherent ground can be found in the work of marxist feminists for constructing a directly revolutionary agency. It is only in so far as they are feminists that they can legitimately rely on a subjective dimension (but which they make exclusively "idealist"). It is not as "marxists" (i.e., scientific social analysts) that they can draw upon their experience in the male world or political organizations. It is only their "feeling/experiencing" selves as feminists that dictate that they should directly do their own politics and oust men (even great male theorists) from the role of representation. But this legitimation on the basis of "feeling/experience" never comes together with their "scientific" and objective economic analysis.[28]

Without a materialist and historical view of consciousness, without a theory of a *conscious* and transformative relation between labour, self and society, the notion of self or subjectivity remains unconnected to social organization or history in any formative and fundamental sense. The "feminist" component of marxist feminism is an uncritical adoption of an essentialist or idealist subjectivist position, just as much as the "marxist" component is an objective idealism. In present-day socialist feminism this dilemma is silenced rather than resolved. And in this diffusion or contradiction between two irreducibly different epistemological positions feminists are seeking — and aided in their compromise by — theories of "difference."

The theory of "difference," and a plea to "diversity" or a tolerant co-existence, has liberated socialist/marxist feminists from the earlier worry about an integrative analysis or theoretical consistency. A text such as *What is Feminism?*, edited by Oakley and Mitchell, both old-time marxists, displays this compromise most effectively in its selection of topics, authors and analysis. "Together we are women," once the trademark of liberal feminists, has appeared in marxist feminism as well —

but interestingly enough, throughout the text the concept "women" (with its diversity) signals mainly to white skin as its boundary and displays the insidiousness of a common sense racism.

## Beyond "The Other(s)," "Identities" and "Structures"

*[People] make their own history, but they do not make it just as they please; they do not make it under circumstances chosen by themselves, but under circumstances directly found, given and transmitted from the past.*

— Karl Marx, *The Eighteenth Brumaire of Louis Bonaparte*

These theories of "other(s)," "identities" and "structures" — all of which contain some truth, and much that is false in them — obviously can not explain my world or meet the pedagogic needs with which my paper started. Subsuming concrete contradictions in an abstraction of essentialism or structuralism, or simultaneously creating multiple subjectivities while enclosing them into static "identities," does not, in the end, create a knowledge that allows us an authenticity of being and politics.

For that, we need to go beyond gestures, signals and constructs, into producing an actively revolutionary knowledge. Here I agree with Marx that we can not be satisfied with simply "interpreting" or presenting different versions (or sub-versions) of the world, we need to change it. It is not enough for us to have the ability, right or space to express ourselves and to describe our experiences. We have to end the oppressive conditions, the social organizations, ultimately not of our own making, which give rise to our experience. We must be simultaneously aware of the cognitive, practical and transformative relation between our consciousness and the world we inhabit. We need to remember that this world into which we are born, or migrate (voluntarily, yet at the pull of capital, or driven by political exigencies), has existed prior to our entry and goes way beyond the local and the immediate. Needless to say it exerts a formative pressure — an objective determination — on us. We are the active-while-acted-upon agents without whom history would be simply reduced to a self-reproducing Hegelian category. So we non-white women, who seek not only to express but to end our oppression, need reliable knowledge which allows us to be actors in history. This knowledge can not be produced in the context of ruling but only in conscious resistance to it. It must retain the integrity of our concrete subject positions within its very project and its present day method of investigation, in so far as it searches the history and social relations to trace the reasons for and the forms of our oppression.

This new theorization must challenge binary or oppositional relations of concepts such as general and particular, subject and object, and display a mediational, integrative, formative or constitutive relation between them which negates such polarization. This could be done by further developing Marx's concept of mediation, displayed and discussed in *Capital* as well as in *Grundrisse*. The sole purpose of the concept is to capture the dynamic, showing how social relations and forms come into being in and through each other, to show how a mode of production is an historically and socially concrete formation. This approach ensures that the integrative actuality of social existence is neither conceptually ruptured and presented fragmentarily nor abstracted into an empty universalism. Neither is there an extrapolation of a single aspect — a part standing in for the whole — nor the whole erasing the parts. Within this framework the knowledge of the social arises in the deconstruction of the concrete into its multiple mediations of social relations and forms which displays "the convergence of many determinations."[29]

This allows us to create a knowledge which provides an approximation between our internal (mental/conceptual) and external reality. Then we can show, through a formative interplay between the subjective and the objective moments — i.e., the particulars of different social relations — how the social and the historical always exist *as* and *in* "concrete" forms of social being and knowing. Our selves and worlds express, embody, encompass and yet extend beyond individual experience, intention and location. Everything that is local, immediate and concrete is thus to be considered as "specific" rather than "particular" — a single entity reveals both its uniqueness and its species nature, that is, its homology with, or typification of, the general. Spacio-temporally it exists here and now, while also acquiring its being in history and the social organization which surrounds it.

I have indicated throughout that we need a reflexive and relational social analysis which incorporates in it a theory of agency and direct representation based on our experience. As such I can directly express what happens to me. But my experience would only be the starting point of my politics. For a further politicization my experience must be recounted within a broader socio-historical and cultural framework that signals the larger social organization and forms which contain and shape our lives. My expressive attempt at description can hold in itself the seeds of an explanation and analysis. We need to go beyond expressive self-referentiality and connect with others in time and space. For this reason, an adequate description of the smallest racist incident leaves room for reference or contextualization to slavery, colonization, imperialism; exploitation of surplus value and construction of the labour market through gender, "race," and ethnicity; nation states to organize and facilitate these processes and practices; and concomitant reifying forms of consciousness.

At this point we must ask the question whether the issue of racism, since we (non-white women) suffer from it, is a so-called "black" issue. The right to express and demand direct representation and to act on racism, and the legitimacy of the different women's groups to be active on this issue, have been the centre of much acrimony and caused divisions. The options are mostly phrased in terms of substitution (white women speak for us) and silence (ours), or direct expression (by us — "White women listen!") and silence (theirs). "You can't speak my reality" has been a strong demand of ours. But in real political terms, are these the only options that face us — those of mutually exclusive agencies? Or must we begin to use my previously suggested integrative and reflexive analysis to work out a political position which allows anyone to speak for/from the experience of individuals and groups while leaving room to speak "socially" from other locations, along the lines of the relations that (in)form our/my own experience?

My emphasis is on the concept "social," which allows many or all to speak about the same problem or reality without saying the same thing. The "social" of course does not always signal empathy, sympathy, agreement and positive cooperation. It includes not only existential similarities but profound contradictions as well. Friends and enemies are constructed by the same ground rules. The social signifiers of an oppressive experience can be "shared" by others who inhabit the same social relations of ruling but benefit from them. Those ruling relations and categories of administration based on imputations of inferiority (physical or cultural) characteristic of racism pervade the whole social space of advanced capitalism. It is as familiar a set of practices and ideas to white people as to non-whites — to the doer and the done unto. As such there is no reason as to why "racism" is solely a "black" experience, though there are different moments and entry points into it, since different aspects of the same social relations are visible at different intersections, from different social locations.

This still does not take away a participant role (willing or unwilling) from either the white or the non-white members of the society. There is always a social and an intellectual possibility for anyone to follow this Ariadne's thread of a relational and reflexive analysis, and thus to go beyond the immediate, through the labyrinth of the mediation and organization of social relations and consciousness to the Minotaur of a post-colonial imperialist capitalism. If that is her issue, then any woman, white or black, can speak to "racism" as "her experience" without substitution, guilt or condescension. Indeed, there are many stories to tell.

In the context of this relational/reflexive social analysis, how must we understand the experience and subjectivity of the knower who is also a political actor? This can only happen if we cut through the false polarity posited between the personal/the private/the individual and the mental, and the social/collective/the public and the political, and find a formative mediation between the two. This calls for a move to revise in marxist terms what "materialism" has crudely meant to some feminist thinking. Defining it in machines and biology, but also valorizing the historical and the social, we can display "being" as "social" being and display the social organization as a subject's creation — as "sensuous, practical, human activities," though not often for herself.

In *The German Ideology* Marx speaks of such a historical-cultural materialism which posits an interconstitutive relation between the mental and the social, implying thought and expression in and as social relations between people, as well as creativity, through the concept of conscious labour. The social is fundamentally communicative and formative and it negates solipsism and autism. That meaning is always implicated in organization and practice as "practical consciousness" becomes evident for Marx through the very existence of language, which is both a result and the condition of being "social." Everything that is "social" then, has a conscious producer or an agent who stands between creating and mediating thought and practice, as simultaneously a bridge between and a source for both the personal and the social.

For an individual, her knowledge, in the immediate sense (which we call "experience") is local and partial. But, nonetheless it is neither "false" nor fantastic. It is more than the raw data of physical reflexes and feelings. It is the originating point of knowledge, an interpretation, a relational sense-making, which incorporates social meaning. This "experience" creates and transforms. It is a continuous process of relating with the world as "our world" (not a "good" world, necessarily). To cut through the conventional dualisms of gender-organized mental and manual labour and their philosophical forms, we would have to recognize and validate our own ability to experience and the experiences themselves as the moments of creativity and the embodiment of formative, rather than dualist, relations. Experience, therefore, is that crucible in which the self and the world enter into a creative union called "social subjectivity."

The role of experience and subjectivity in the production of "scientific" knowledge and revolutionary politics has been controversial among academics and orthodox marxists. Even the socialist or marxist feminists have not given centrality to the experiencing subject (outside of her/his economic functions). The major tendency has been to rely on "scientific" political economy and to dismiss experience and subjectivity as an outgrowth of bourgeois individualism and psychologism. It is mainly in marxist cultural theory, preoccupied with problems of representation and materialism in culture, and in marxist phenomenology and work based on that of Antonio Gramsci, that we find theorizations validating experience/subjectivity. In these traditions, a concept of direct and creative agency is built into the process and content of knowledge. Here experience acts as a fulcrum or a hinge from which we can turn both inward and outward.

A very significant use of "experience" (perhaps the most extended attempt) in the marxist feminist tradition is in the work of Dorothy E. Smith. Here it is less theorized in terms of *what experience is*, but more methodologically used for *what it does* in organizing a social inquiry.[30] It is not treated by her as world view or a body of content as much as a set of social relations, and disjunctive relations at that, within the social organization for ruling (us). Thus it serves as the point of departure for investigation, and is deconstructively employed. It is a (woman) subject's immediate and lived (as interpreted) experience of herself and the world she happens to be in which simultaneously positions her as a knower-subject and a social-object of research. Entitled "social organization of knowledge," Smith's method provides us with a critique of the discourse of Cartesian rationalism and of the mental and manual division of labour as social (institutional) and conceptual practices of power. Disclosing the bourgeois ideological and patriarchal character of this discourse by entering it from the woman's standpoint, Smith establishes the validity of beginning from the local and the immediate — namely, our experience — in order to explore the larger social organization.

This historical materialist understanding of experience, which treats it as an interpretive relation rather than valorizing any person's or group's experience as a repository of "truth," provides a possible active knowledge apparatus.[31] We retain through this combination both our direct agency and our representation as knowers and practitioners but also can achieve a validated status for our experience which contains the potential for revolutionary knowledge.

In this theorization experience is not understood as a body of content indicative of a seamless subjectivity or psychological totalization, but rather as a subject's attempt at sense-making. Using it, we, non-white women, can begin to use our alienating experiences in classrooms as the point of departure or a set of references for a comprehensive social analysis. Any such experience of alienation holds in it the double awareness of being "self" and the "other," our personal and public modes of being. From this vantage point the social relations and discursive practices of our classrooms become visible as practices and discourses of domination, otherization and objectification. We see how conventional social theories, for example, have, without malice or intention, built into them alienating forms and ideas which distance us from ourselves as social subjects.

The social analysis we need, therefore, must begin from *subjectivity*, which asserts dynamic, contradictory and unresolved dimensions of experience and consequently does not reify itself into a fixed psychological category called *identity* which rigidifies an individual's relationship with her social environment and history. Subjectivity and experience, understood in this way, argue for a coherence of feeling and being without forcing either a homogeneity on or a fragmentation of subjectivity, as advocated by post-modernism. Since political agency, experience and knowledge are transformatively connected, where but in ourselves and lives can we begin our explanatory and analytical activities? On what but our authentic subjectivity can we lay the foundations of a revolutionary politics? This renders the talk of "false consciousness" redundant and rather signals a beginning in what Gramsci called "the twilight zone of commonsense."

A socialist revolution is obviously not to the taste of everybody nor a matter of civil rights, but if the fundamental need for a just, equitable and humane society is to be granted any legitimacy at all, we cannot but seek the eradication of the social organization that produces alienation and domination. This eradication cannot be truly achieved through spontaneous insurrections, visions and uncensored expressions. We need a social analysis whose theory and practice involve political actors who both produce this knowledge and make it organizationally actionable. Its task in the Canadian context is to uncover the norms and forms of imperialist capitalism which organize our social space and individual experiences. Such a revolutionary knowledge cannot but be anti-racist/anti-imperialist, and cannot be created outside of the experiences and representation of non-white women. This does not mean an ontological privileging of any individual non-white woman's personal experiences and views as "the truth" about society, but rather using these many truths, descriptions of differences, as the widest point of entry into a social analysis of mediation of those social relations — encoded as gender, race and class. This allows us a convergence of existence with theory and method and of experience with politics. And it is toward this ideal that I grope, both as a student and a teacher — a praxis born out of our humble lives as non-white women living in the jungle of an advanced capitalist society.

## Endnotes

1. Presidency College was one of the earliest colleges established by the British in India (Calcutta) during the colonial era, early in the nineteenth century. Richardson was a renowned professor of English literature at this college.

2. McCaulay, in a now famous Minute to the British Parliament in 1835, urged: "We must do our best to form a class who may be interpreters between us and the millions whom we govern...a class of persons, Indian in blood and colour but English in taste, in opinions, in morals and in intellect." Quoted in S.K.Chatterjee, *English Education in India* (Delhi: MacMillan Company of India, 1976), p. 58.

3. The notion of "sexist racism" first attracted my attention in two essays in *The Empire Strikes Back* (London: Hutchinson, 1982). See Hazel V. Carby, "White Women Listen! Black feminism and the boundaries of Sisterhood" (pp. 212-235), and Pratibha Parmar, "Gender, race and class: Asian women's resistance" (pp. 236-275). See also Himani Bannerji, "Popular Images of South Asian Women," *Parallelogram* (Vol. 2, No. 4, 1986).

4. For a discussion on the politics of International Women's Day and the March 8th Coalition, see Carolyn Egan, Linda Lee Gardiner and Judy Vashti Persad, "The Politics of Transformation: Struggles with Race, Class and Sexuality in the March 8th Coalition" (pp. 20-47) in *Feminism and Political Economy: Women's Work, Women's Struggles* (Toronto: Methuen, 1987).

5. See Himani Bannerji, "Introducing Racism: Notes Towards an Anti-Racist Feminism" in *Resources for Feminist Research* (Vol. 16, No. 1, 1987).

6. John Berger, *Ways of Seeing* (London: BBC, 1972). An essential reading on cultural commonsense, especially the essay on "The Nude."

7. See Paolo Freire, *The Pedagogy of the Oppressed* (New York: Continuum, 1970).

8. See Dorothy E. Smith, "A Sociology for Women," "Institutional Ethnography: A Feminist Research," and other essays in *The Everyday World as Problematic: A Feminist Sociology* (Toronto: University of Toronto Press, 1987).

9. For the concept of mediation, understood in a marxist sense, see Raymond Williams, *Marxism and Literature* (Oxford: Oxford University Press, 1977)and *Keywords* (London: Flamingo, 1983), and Marx himself in *Grundrisse* (Middlesex: Penguin, 1973). This has been a key concept in marxist cultural theory, but increasingly important in social theory.

10. Though Simone de Beauvoir's *The Second Sex* (New York: Vintage, 1974) has been lumped together with the work of other essentialist feminists, it is not quite of the same philosophical and political persuasion. Marxist phenomenological feminism of de Beauvoir with a historicized notion of "patriarchy" is a far cry from Millett, Friedan, etc.

11. For a clear view of "patriarchy" as re-interpreted by liberal and radical feminists, see Kate Millet's *Sexual Politics* (London: Sphere, 1971) or Andrea Dworkin's *Pornography* (New York: William Morrow, 1980).

12. See Angela Miles, "Feminist Radicalism in the 1980s" in *Canadian Journal of Political and Social Theory: Feminism Now* (Vol. Nos. 1-2, 1985). Her full statement on this issue sums up the stand of many others, and particularly rests on the theory of "essentially" different male/female consciousnesses propounded by Mary O'Brien in *The Politics of Reproduction* (1981), based on "their materially different experience of the process of reproduction" (quoted by Miles, p. 21).

Miles' own statement is worth quoting: "...unless one accepts *the sociobiological or liberal notion of innately aggressive and competitive, acquisitive man* it must remain problematic why the existence of surplus and other resources for domination are actually used by some to dominate others." (p. 18, emphasis mine) Miles' and O'Brien's ahistorical use of the concept of materialism to develop an essentialist perspective base on a biological or other *innate human nature* argument is different from the use of the concept in marxist terms, as in the anthology edited by Annette Kuhn and Ann Marie Wolpe, *Feminism and Materialism* (London: Routledge & Kegan Paul, 1978), but is used earlier by Shulamith Firestone in *The Dialectic of Sex* (New York: William Morrow, 1970). Whereas the Kuhn and Wolpe collection has little historical perspective, it interprets the notion of the "material" to mean a "social" perspective rather than a biological/physical one. An interesting, though quite erroneous reading of materialism and marxism in an essentialist context comes out in Nancy Hartsock's *Money, Sex and Power: Toward a Feminist Historical Materialism* (Boston: Northeastern University Press, 1984). She claims that "[Women's] experience and relation with others, with the natural world, of mind and body — *provide an ontological base for developing a nonproblematic social synthesis....* (p. 246, emphasis mine). For a critique of Hartsock's essentialism see M. Kline, "Women's Oppression and Racism: A Critique of the 'Feminist Standpoint.'" in *Race, Class, Gender: Bonds and Barriers* (Toronto: Between the Lines, 1989).

13. See Tania Das Gupta's introduction to *Race, Class, Gender* (Toronto: Between the Lines, 1989) on "white middleclass women pretending to speak for all women," p. 1.

14. Elizabeth Spelman, *Inessential Woman* (Boston: Beacon Press, 1988), p. 13.

15. "Paradoxically, in feminist theory it is a refusal to take differences among women seriously that lies at the heart of feminism's implicit politics of domination...." Spelman, *op. cit.*, p. 11. For

an example of such "a refusal" to see real differences among women, especially white and non-white women, see particularly the introduction of *The Politics of Diversity* (Boston: Beacon Press, 1986). On different approaches to the question of difference see also *Discovering Reality*, Sandra Harding and Merrill B. Hintikka, ed. (Dordrecht, Holland: D. Reidel, 1983) and *The Future of Difference*, Hester Eisentein and Alice Jardine, ed. (New Brunswick: Rutgers University Press, 1985), among many other anthologies (some included in the bibliography). The politics of "difference" ranges from neo-pluralism of "diversity" to a more radical insistence on relations of power, of which good examples are writings by bell hooks, Trinh T. Minh-ha, or even the philosopher Spelman, or the literary critic Toril Moi. Sandra Harding, however, would fall within the "diversity" tradition.

16. For powerful examples of Black and Asian women's protest see *The Empire Strikes Back* (London: Hutchinson, 1982) and many others in the U.S. and U.K. The theoretical range lies between marxism (Angela Davis) and radicalism (bell hooks).

17. See Toril Moi's "Virginia Woolf" in *Canadian Journal of Political and Social Theory* (Vol. 9, Nos. 1-2, 1985), where she critiques a "humanist, totalizing aesthetics" and politics and speaks for changing subject positions and related politics both among and within subjects. For her and others, we need to "radically undermine the notion of the unitary self" and give up "the search for a unifed individual identity (or gender identity) or indeed a 'textual identity.'" Any other approach is "highly reductive and selective" (pp. 137-139). Also in this context of de-centering see Pamela McCallum's "Woman as Ecriture or Woman as Other" in *Ibid*.

18. A good case in point is Trinh T. Minh-ha's new book, *Woman, Native, Other* (Bloomington: Indiana University Press, 1989), which on the one hand carefully outlines the objectification of Third

World women through colonial discourse, but considers this domination at the level of discourse alone.

19. This is so pervasive that it defies listing. However, a few representative texts of political economy of Canadian women will indicate the absence that I notice. *Women at Work*, Acton, et. al., ed. (Toronto: Canadian Women's Educational Press, 1974), *Still Ain't Satisfied*, FitzGerald, et. al., ed. (Toronto: Women's Press, 1982), *Feminism and Political Economy: Women's Work, Women's Struggles*, Heather Jon Maroney and Meg Luxton, ed. (Toronto: Methuen, 1987) will give an idea of the "race blindness" I speak of, and how simplistically class and gender are conceived when understood outside of the practices of colonialism, imperialism and Canadian capitalism and their attendant racist discourse and commonsense. Also see *What is Feminism?* Juliet Mitchell and Ann Oakley, ed. (New York: Pantheon, 1986), throughout the introduction of which everything is spoken of but racism or the particularities of the lives of non-white women in the U.K., U.S. and Canada. Any talk of "working class women," failing this contextualization, is mere empty rhetoric. In the Canadian context, see the separate and marginal role of "women of colour" in *Feminist Organizing for Change* Nancy Adamson, Linda Briskin and Margaret McPhail (Toronto: Oxford University Press, 1988).

20. See Meg Luxton's *More Than a Labour of Love* (Toronto: Women's Press, 1980) for a humane example of this approach. Speaking of nuclear households and seeing them primarily as sites of "domestic labour," she formulates the everyday life at home in terms of "labour process." As she puts it, a household is "...a *production process* that is conducted between two arenas of economic exchange — the labour or job market and the consumer goods market." (p. 16) See also *Hidden in the Household*, Bonnie Fox, ed. (Toronto: Women's Press, 1980), for "value" production at home and a discussion on "domestic labour."

21. Books such as *Double Ghetto*, Pat Armstrong and Hugh

Armstrong (Toronto: McClelland and Stewart, 1978), for example, would call for such an overview and specificity, from the logic of the text itself, which calls for a materialist (i.e., historical and social) analysis of organization of labour by Canadian capital. The inability of political economy to come to terms with racism, for example, is noticed by Dorothy Smith in her comment on feminism's uncritical acceptance of its conventional reifying discourse. "The contours of the discursive barriers are perhaps most strikingly displayed in our failure as feminists working within the political economic tradition of racism implicit in our practices and arising less from attitudes we hold as individuals as from just the ways that we participate in and practice the discursive assumptions and the structuring of the 'main business' within the relations of ruling." See Smith, "Feminist Reflections on Political Economy" in *Studies in Political Economy* (Autumn 1989), p. 53.

22. See Pat Armstrong and M. Patricia Connelly, "Feminist Political Economy: An Introduction" in *Studies in Political Economy* (Autumn 1989). "In our view, class has to be reconceptualized through race and gender within regional, national and international contexts. The static categorizing of class that has been used in so much of class analysis does not capture the experience of gender, race/ethnicity or class." (p. 5) This statement draws our attention to the same lack that I speak about, to be found throughout in feminist political economy. See also the introduction to Barrett and Hamilton's *The Politics of Diversity* (London: Verso, 1986) and its view of Canada as an entity of two nations, Anglo-French, even though a token "politically correct" gesture is made to the plight of the Native Peoples of Canada. Roxana Ng, in her essay "Sexism, racism, nationalism" in *Race, Class, Gender* (Toronto: Between the Lines, 1989), comments on the racist character of this type of historiography.

23. An interesting example of this *structural* understanding comes out in the domestic labour formulations. Meg Luxton's *More Than a Labour of Love* begins by stating: "Housewives make up

one of the largest *occupational* groups in Canada" (p. 11) and goes on to speak of the four structures or "distinct work processes" of a household, "*each* composed of a variety of tasks and *each having its own history*, its own internal rythms and pressures and its own particular patterns of change" (p. 19 emphases mine).

24. See *Women and Revolution: A Discussion of the Unhappy Marriage of Marxism and Feminism*, Lydia Sargent, ed. (Boston: South End Press, 1981). In her introductory piece, "New Left Women and Men: The Honeymoon is Over," Sargent speaks in terms of "the problem of day to day work (who cleans the office...etc.)" and "the problem of theory (who leads the revolution...etc.)," outlining the dilemma for women of the left of "going or staying" as experientially determined. In Sargent's analysis, "who" or the agency and experience are central but not thought out, and nowhere does she question the type of marxism practiced by the male left. Instead we only hear "who leads the revolution," etc.

25. "Feminist Reflections," (p. 53) in *Studies in Political Economy* (1989).

26. See Heidi Hartman, "The Unhappy Marriage of Marxism and Feminism: Towards a more progressive union" in *Women and Revolution* (1981). "The marriage of Marxism and feminism has been like the marriage of husband and wife depicted in English common law, Marxism and feminism are one, and that one is Marxism. Recent attempts to integrate Marxism and feminism are unsatisfactory to us as feminists because they subsume the feminist struggle into the 'larger' struggle against capital" (p. 2).

27. Karl Marx, *The Critique of German Ideology* (New York: International Publishers, 1970).

28. Hartman or Sargent, or Zillah Eisenstein in *Capitalist Patriarchy and the Case for Socialist Feminism* (New York and London: Monthly Review Press, 1979), are powerful examples of this

divided intellect and self as marxists and feminists, and concomitantly of separate conceptions of gender and class as two separate social categories to be added up together. Gloria Joseph, in "The Incompatible Menage a Trois: Marxism, Feminism and Racism," in *Women and Revolution* (1981), remarks on this separation.

29. Karl Marx, *Grundrisse* (1973), p. 93.

30. See Dorothy E. Smith, "A Sociology for Women," in *The Everyday World as Problematic* (Toronto: University of Toronto Press, 1987).

31. See E.P.Thompson, *The Poverty of Theory and Other Essays* (New York and London: Monthly Review Press, 1978).

≈   # Subjects of Discourse: Learning the Language That Counts [1]

*by Kate McKenna*
. . . . . . . . . . . . . . . . . . . . . . . . . . . . . .

My interest in this collaboration grew out of the tensions and contradictions I feel about my own location and participation in "higher education." As an undergraduate women's studies student and more recently as a graduate student, there have been times when I have found myself intrigued, stimulated, inspired — sensing the possibilities opened by certain pedagogic practices and avenues of inquiry. But more often I have been overwhelmed by feelings of alienation, anger and dismay at the disjuncture between the kinds of environments and interactions which I have come to understand to be essential for active and transformative learning,[2] and the social relations that we enter into and produce through academic training and discursive practices.[3]

I have been particularly disturbed by the lack of space, discourse, and/or "permission" to take up these tensions and contradictions in higher education as points of entry and areas for exploration. That feminist/critical pedagogy, when it is addressed within academia, is most often treated as some "thing" that we students are being trained to do somewhere else, to Other people, seems deeply flawed. Although much of the literature on the subject may advocate taking the problems and everyday social relations of the students and teachers themselves as a starting point for inquiry (Ellsworth, 1989; Freire, 1970; Giroux, 1988), my classroom experiences suggest that within institutions of "higher learning" this is a practice which is often strongly resisted by professors and students alike. Perhaps not unrelated is that some people have warned me that it may actually be dangerous to my academic future to focus directly on academic training as an area for research. Although they are not usually named as such, I have begun to think of experiences like these — these kinds of resistance, these warnings — as being very much part of my academic training. For if academic discursive practices, as practices of governance, are accomplished as much by style and form as by content, then these everyday experiences can be read as signals marking the ideological boundaries of the institutionalized academic frame. It is these boundaries that I want to explore. I take seriously Corrigan's point that "what we have to do — this 'we' being located individuals like myself within the apparatus of education — is to start examining *where we are.* How do 'our' neutral, natural, universal and Obvious forms operate, what is their differential impact, how are we embodied in them, what do they encourage and what do they deny?" (1984:20-22). In writing this paper as part of that work in progress, I began to try and clarify how this project has taken root in my own concerns as a learner. I think it is important to share a little of that history.


Where to begin...
    Although I had been in and out of university classrooms over a number of years, what I think of as my "real education" developed as I became politically active. I remember a number of things that contributed to this shift in my life. As I worked alone in a small pottery studio in rural Nova Scotia, I would listen to CBC radio. I heard the news, or variations of it, over and over again — hour after hour, day after day. Over time I began to recognize patterns in how information was being put together. I started to see how the events were always disconnected from each other, from their historical sequence and from

the people who may have been visible in them days or even hours previously. I became more and more frustrated by the way "two sides" of the issue — the construction of media "objectivity" — limited what could be known or discussed. I began to notice and appreciate voices that spoke with *feeling* and also noticed how rarely they were given space. I became familiar with how much more time got alloted to representatives of status quo positions and with how interviewers would use different tones of voice and interviewing techniques to either grant credibility or question legitimacy.

I started to talk about this with friends, to share what I had heard, my pain and horror at what was happening in the world around me, connections I was making between the stories, my growing conviction that we had a responsibility not only to become informed but to respond. On my bulletin board I keep a cartoon to remind me of this time. It is a line drawing by Halifax artist Dawna Gallager showing three people seated around a table. The caption reads: "Ruining dinner by discussing reality." For many friends, my developing political analysis and enthusiasm were disconcerting. To talk about these issues created rifts between us. I felt their anger. My growing politicization brought our social location into view — something which is often strongly resisted by "...middle-class white people, who would just like to 'be', unconstrained by labels, by identities, by consignment to a group, and would prefer to ignore the fact that their [/our] existence and social place are anything other than self-evident, natural, human" (Martin and Mohanty, 1987:206).

But, fortunately, I also began to locate people with whom I could share impressions, information and anger. We began to act as reality checks for each other: "Did you hear what they said on the seven a.m. news? Did you notice that by eight a.m. they had cut it?" "Do you know they had someone on the afternoon show today arguing for uranium mining — saying that the health hazards were less than eating peanut butter on a regular basis?" The inevitable question arose: What can I do?

I began to read in a purposeful way, to attend lectures, meetings and rallies and participated in a workshop on non-violent direct action. In June 1983, after months of listening to discussions and reading about Solicitor General Robert Kaplan's proposed bill to establish a civilian security intelligence agency (CSIS) and finding that no one was working on a response locally, I organized a lunch hour demonstration. From that first inititative things snowballed and I found myself working non-stop for the next year and a half. This involved many different kinds of activities. I found others who were interested in initiating and organizing various local and regional demonstrations and conferences. A group of us formed a women's action affinity group in which we collectively wrote and performed street theatre pieces. Working on press releases, pamphlets, newspaper articles and speeches, I began to improve my writing skills. I learned about different resources for popular education and used them to facilitate community education about the connections between militarism, imperialism and other forms of domination. Some of us organized a study group. It was a stimulating time, filled with challenging learning experiences.

This period of my life ended when my male partner was offered a job teaching in Whitedog, one of two Ojibway communities in Northwestern Ontario devastated by the mercury poisoning of the English and Wabigoon River systems. With our move to this community another period of learning began, one which radically challenged the authority of much that I had come to *know*, and which taught me why I must constantly struggle to *learn how to know differently*.

Day-to-day experiences living as a white woman in a First Nations' community taught me that the intellectual solidarity and theoretical analysis of racism and of white supremacist imperialism which I had arrived with were valuable but only as a starting point. Two years in Whitedog challenged my way of viewing myself, shifting the focus of my political activism and of what I perceived as possible strategies for change. For these and other reasons, I was somewhat apprehensive when, during our first winter in the community, I was contacted by Nova Scotian women who were organizing an international women's peace conference. They invited me to attend the conference and asked me to approach one of the Ojibway women I was becoming friends with to invite her to accompany me and to speak at the conference. Unfortunately my feelings of apprehension proved to be well-founded.

My friend had been asked to speak on a panel focusing on the question "How does the arms race affect women?" She had told me she does not like to speak in public and was concerned that by doing so she might risk losing her job — at the time she had been the community health worker for over fifteen years. However, in the end she said that her deep concern for the future of her children and grandchildren and her dreams for some security in her community overweighed this reluctance and she decided to speak.

When she addressed the women at the conference, she told us that nuclear war was *not* the immediate concern in her community. She talked about the environmental damage, the mercury poisoning of the river system that had been the life blood of the community for generations. She spoke of the flooding by Ontario Hydro of traditional rice fields and burial grounds and of the uranium mining that was killing the earth and her people. These immediate and basic problems, the social results of which she was dealing with on a daily basis, were what she tried to communicate.

But, when the chance came for conference participants to address the panel, which included a Filipina woman as well as a woman working in Ethiopia, not one question was directed to my friend. Although suggestions were made about what we or our government should do about situations of oppression in the Philippines, Ethiopia, and South Africa, not one of us mentioned that we needed to press the Canadian government about First Nations' land claims or their struggle for self-government. The only woman who did address a comment to my Ojibway friend was able to tell her, with impunity, that if she "really cared" about the future of her grandchildren she had to be concerned with Star Wars. Her comments echoed words I had heard spoken by another white Canadian woman the day before in a different workshop: "*We* have allowed them to have their say, now they have to let *us* get on with what *we* are here for."

At the time I felt deep sadness and shame at what had taken place. The violence I saw happening in the interaction with my friend was not done by women who disassociate themselves from political involvement but by white feminists who had been invited to participate in the conference because of their activism — some of them women I had worked closely with before moving to Whitedog. In an article I wrote shortly after, I said that I could only wish the conference translation service had been up to the task of bridging the gap that would have been necessary to make this Ojibway woman's message comprehensible to the privileged white women she addressed. However, re-reading the article now, from this distance and with a keener appreciation of language as a site of political struggle, I recognize that although I suggested at the time that the lack of communication was *connected* with differences in resources and privilege, I did not identify this communication as a particular kind of *discursive practice*, as an instance illuminating what Edward Said meant when he said "...far from being a type of conversation between equals, the discursive is more usually like the unequal relation between colonizer and colonized, oppressor and oppressed" (1982:48).

I am trying to excavate — and struggle against — the ways "scholarly" conventions of academic writing enter into and produce these same kinds of discursive relations. Taken-for-granted "scholarly" practices encourage academics to treat other people's words and experiences as resources which can be selectively organized to illustrate predetermined conceptual frameworks (Smith, 1990). Besides having little to do with the actual concerns and experiences of the people who are written about, using conceptual frameworks in this way expresses and produces oppressive race, gender and class relations. The institutionalization of practices of racism, sexism and class power within practices of "scholarship" has insured that "academic freedom" in capitalist societies has never been a serious threat. A broad range of studies can be pursued within educational institutions; yet those explorations are regulated and encapsulated by "proper forms of academic expression," which are already "valued" (Corrigan, 1981).

Corrigan has argued that "through the enforced modalities of a required, encouraged, rewarded discursivity, we have been colonized (and subsequently have become the colonizer)" (quoted in Lewis and Simon, 1986:468). The way I saw my friend being silenced and made Other by what was and was not said that day is not an unusual occurrence. There are methods of speaking, ways of using language which work as procedures of domination, and which both produce and enter people into ruling relations (Smith, 1979; 1989).

At various times during the conference it was painfully obvious how, in using various political/theoretical frameworks, white women can, however unintentionally, enter into and produce a standpoint which exists within extended relations of ruling. White Western feminist writings on "peace" organized a genre of feminist speech and writing in which the problems and experiences of a particular group of women were constructed as being everywoman's problems, and then presented as priorities around which all women were expected to organize (Bannerji, 1987; Mohanty, 1988; Spelman, 1988). At the same time, these discursive practices suppressed and silenced the concerns and experiences of large numbers of women, constituting them as Other. In conferences, classrooms and academic texts there are numerous examples of how white academics continue to speak a racist discourse perhaps without "meaning to do so." These practices of discursive imperialism are part of what I have been trying to grapple with.

In her essay "Introducing Racism: Notes Towards an Anti-

Racist Feminism," Himani Bannerji (1987) talks about the norms and forms of racism that are embedded in everyday habits and ways of thinking — practices which are so pervasive she refers to them as "common sense racism." She says:

>...Whereas clearly stated racism definitely exists, the more problematic aspect for us is this common sense racism which holds the norms and forms thrown up by a few hundred years of pillage, extermination, slavery, colonization and neo-colonization. It is in these diffused normalized sets of assumptions, knowledge, and so-called cultural practices that we come across racism in its most powerful, because pervasive, form.
>
>These norms and forms...produce silences or absences, creating gaps and fissures through which non-white women, for example, disappear from the social surface. Racism becomes an everyday life and "normal" way of seeing. (1987:11)

Returning to university as a "mature" student in the summer of 1986, I quickly became aware of the real limitations of the form, language and subject matter which are required from a student/academic in order to be taken "seriously." These academic practices encourage and normalize particular ways of giving meaning to the world while at the same time actively supressing alternative interpretations. I understood that I was being trained and socialized to communicate with and within the terms of the dominant institutions. What is more important, I knew from my political involvement and time in an Ojibway community that many people were challenging the violence done by these institutional practices to "other kinds of knowledge and other forms of expression which schooling systematically denies, dilutes, down values and distorts" (Corrigan, 1987:22).

Chandra Mohanty points out that "Western feminist scholarship...must be seen and examined precisely in terms of its inscription in particular relations of power and struggle"

(1988:65). I have been trying to understand the ways in which dominant discursive practices in the academy — claims of rationalism, common interest, responsibility, equality, reasonableness, the mental/manual division of labour, reification — are used to maintain existing gender, race and class relations. How does "proper academic training" encourage people to engage in discursive practices which work to regulate communication and to suppress the experiences and challenges of women and other Others? How does "...rational deliberation, reflection, and consideration of all viewpoints ... become a vehicle for regulating conflict and the power to speak, for transforming conflict into rational argument by means of universalized capacities for language and reason" (Ellsworth, 1989:301)? These are questions I continue to struggle with.

I suspect that part of the answer to these questions requires that we "discover" academic training — and Western feminist scholarship — as historically constructed practices within specific relations of power. When I suggest that higher education needs to be examined as a site of "state formation," I am not refering to "the state" as a structure or object which has developed above individuals, but as a complex set of social relations — ongoing practices that people enter into and produce through their activities which, like all human activity, have a particular spatial and temporal character, but which no single person initiates or completes (Foucault, 1982; Smith, 1987). Taking up Foucault's very broad understanding of "government" shifts the focus from relationships between individuals or groups, to looking at how "certain actions may structure the field of other possible actions" (Foucault, 1982:791). Our need for, and the possibility of, this expanded conceptual understanding of ruling, corresponds to a shift in dominant practices. In this sense I agree with Foucault that "the political, ethical, social, philosophical problem of our day is not to try to liberate the individual from the state and from the state's institutions but to liberate us both from the state and from the type of individualization which is linked to the state" (Foucault 1982:785).

We (both teachers and students) become the starting point for analyzing how our educational practices are both constituted by and constitutive of ongoing relations of power. This "suggests looking at the way the dominant ideology is inscribed in the form and content of the classroom material, the organization of the school, the daily classroom social relationships, the principles that structure the selection and organization of the curriculum, the discourse and practices of even those who appear to have penetrated (sic) the ideology's logic" (Giroux, 1981:16).

During my first term at graduate school I attended a one-day popular education workshop. What happened that day helped me become more conscious of the significance of what does and does not get said, what gets written down and what does not, and how these work to structure possibilities for understanding and action. By reflecting on what happened during the workshop, I also gained a better understanding of my own training in practices of self-governance.

The workshop facilitators used a process which was intended to encourage participation. The group was to work together to construct a drawing that addressed some issue we wanted to plan action around. Many times during the day we were encouraged to participate either by making suggestions about what needed to be included in the picture or by physically taking part in constructing the drawing.

We decided to focus on the problem of establishing a women's community health centre, a project in which two of the workshop participants were already involved. As our picture began to develop, one of the women in the group brought up the issue of abortion. She said that she certainly would not be able to support a clinic in her community if it performed or helped women gain access to abortions. The facilitator, who up to this point had been using our talk to add to the images, steered the conversation in another direction and did not include the abortion issue in the drawing.

It became clear, during a small group discussion at the end of the day, that this had been a pivotal point for many of us. It had changed the way we experienced the rest of the day as well as the possibilities afforded by this process of analysis. We had individually registered that this topic was not allowed to enter the picture. As we talked together we concluded that this omission would adversely affect the usefulness of the analysis we had constructed since conflicts about abortion were certainly political realities that the women would come up against in practice.

As we shared our reflection some women began to express their anger about the facilitator. They blamed him for "bad facilitation" or suggested he had a "hidden agenda." While this may well have been part of the interaction, I sensed that what had happened was much more complex and contradictory. My own understanding of the day, as well as experiences in other learning sites, caused me to question how my own/our activities contributed to bringing about these interactions, to look at my own/our tendency to defer to "authority" — to him as a male, to see him as the leader, teacher, and/or expert of the workshop, to question my/our reluctance to take up his often repeated invitation to "define our own agenda," to draw the world from our own experience, to challenge or change the picture we were constructing. I suspected that as participants we had all been fairly well trained in numerous and various practices of self-governance and that that training does not get undone quickly no matter how good the teacher/facilitator or how "participatory" the process.

I have tried to use these insights to think about the pictures I am participating in constructing in my academic training. I have begun to investigate what I and others write down, what gets recorded and what doesn't, what can and can't be discussed. After this workshop I began to keep a journal. This is where I keep field notes about what I learn. Through these notes

I have been exploring the ways that certain social relations and structurings, particularly within institutions of "higher learning," come to limit our knowing and communication as women, as feminists concerned with critical consciousness and social change. In these notebooks I dialogue with others who I encounter through my readings, pulling out bits that speak to my present experience and struggles. In them I record incidents/instances from classroom interactions — moments of significant learning, struggle, and/or points of disjuncture. In the process I have become much more aware of "particulars" that until recently I did not "pull out" and inscribe in the notes/accounts of my classroom learning.

**Field Notes**

*I am reading a geneology of the discursive practices which organized Victorian "civilization" so that "[t]here might be many stages of social evolution and many seemingly bizarre customs and "superstitions" in the world, but there was only one 'civilization,' one path of 'progress,' one 'true religion'" when I come upon Livingston's words about the African's need for "contact with superior races" (Brantlinger, 1985:166-78).*

The production of "self-regulating" individuals through contact with superior ways of reasoning has been a central task for educational institutions. Livingston's words raise questions about whether parallels can be drawn with current discursive practices which organize "academic excellence" and "scholarly practices" of knowing, about the ways academic practices work to construct a "civilized mind."

I have found it disturbing that while some progressive academics currently embrace the importance of critiquing and resisting racist and/or sexist discourse (at least in theory), they rarely problematize the elitist practices and division of labour which produce "superior thinkers" and "proper scholarly practices of conceptualizing" in their own workplaces. My experiences as a student have made me want to explore some of the ways particular ideological practices remain inscribed in "the discourse and practices of those who appear to have penetrated (sic) the ideology's logic" (Giroux, 1981:16). In doing so I want to question the assumption that "penetrating the logic" will fundamentally challenge or change *how* the dominant discursive practices are actually put together.

I think we need to examine the educational practices through which "rational thinkers" are trained/constructed. How is it that thinking and mental production have come to be specialized practices which are separated not only from manual labour but from actual people? How do these practices of knowledge-making produce the social position of middle class white people as obvious, natural, human? What are the social relations that enable such practices to continue? Are these conceptual practices self-validating?

One of the most useful and pervasive myths of liberal capitalism is the belief in the democratizing function of education. Assumptions about how individuals from oppressed groups or progressive movements can benefit from the opportunities offered by *higher* education — by the intellectual appropriation of "the master's tools" (Lorde, 1984) — are rarely made problematic. June Jordan points out that "[n]ot too many people [have] wanted to grant that maybe schools really are political institutions teaching power to the powerful and something unpalatable and self-destructive to the weak" (1989:128). Academics on the left who share this analysis have argued that part of the work of public schooling in capitalist societies has been the reproduction of *difference*. However, they seldom push the analysis further by explicating their own positions and activities in institutions of "higher learning." Rarely do we examine the problem of how, in the process of intellectual appropriation within these elite institutions, certain "neutral" and "obvious" academic practices construct an imaginary symmetrization in which members of all classes appear, and are treated as though, they occupy a *common* position in relation to each other and the state (Curtis, 1983; Wilden, 1980).

**Field Notes**

> *In her essay "Canadian public policy: the unequal structure of representation," Rianne Mahon describes the work the federal Department (sic) of Labour does to encourage the development of "responsible" behaviour among trade unions. She points out that unlike the minister of industry, who speaks explicitly for the manufacturing sector, the job of the minister of labour involves acting as a "go-between" in order to bring about a realization of "common interest" (1977:186-7). It is understood that, within the rubric of common interest, "responsible behaviour" means that unions will structure their demands so that they can "be met within the framework of capitalist relations of production" (Mahon, 1977:186).*

I am beginning to think that in some respects the work of the teacher/academic is often similar. Their jobs are not to speak, or do work explicitly for the subjects of discourse but rather to act as "go-betweens" between actual people and the authorized objectified discourse, to become "a means through which these objectified modes of ruling are passed on" (Smith, 1989). They too must work to bring about an understanding of "common interest" by facilitating a reasonable discourse which will attest to "co-existence being possible despite opposing views" (Carty and Brand, 1988:41). In part a teacher's work involves processes which encourage the development of "responsible" student/academic practices, and discourage those that are not.

The "intentionality" of such projects does not always have to be inferred; at times what is being done is stated quite clearly. For example, Dorothy Smith adds this footnote to her acknowledgement that in the process of her academic training in sociology she "...had learned to be 'responsible'"(1989:37): "Indeed my dissertation supervisor compared me favorably to other women who had dropped out of the Ph.D. program at Berkeley (largely because of the systematic but impalpable discouragement they experienced) telling me that the difference between myself and other women graduate students was that I was "responsible" (Smith, 1989:60)

## Field Notes

*During the final session of one course, the weekly readings were set aside in order to discuss how the class could respond to a text which has caused pain and anger in the Native community. The discussion raised themes that had been the focus of the course: the possibility of multiple interpretations, redeeming features of the text, desire for the text, the economic text, censorship, insurgent readings and so forth. As the instructor was filling the board with these concepts, a Native woman in the class suggested that with all of our discussion and "rationalizing" we were getting farther and farther away from dealing with the problem of the racism in the text.*

*The way in which the particular discursive practices that we were being taught in this class worked as a form of governance became obvious to me when I saw how her insight was written as text on the board. What she had said did not get recorded as "the problem of racism" or "the problem of rationalizing" but became reconstructed by the instructor as "the problem of good/bad constructions."*

I need to be mindful of how, within this capitalist patriarchy, training in the practices of academic scholarship, even feminist scholarship, may serve to legitimize the illegitimate. How do various discursive practices within the academy limit possibilities for taking up and confronting racism, sexism and other everyday experiences of oppression as they are practiced within institutions of higher learning?

One of the ways I see this working is through a process of political de-legitimation in which, in becoming trained as academics we are encouraged to participate in various discursive practices which exclude all but the initiated, the chosen few. Through this process "critical thinking" is transformed into a scholarly activity which is legitimized and sanitized in so far as it remains disconnected from actual political activity and disappears from popular view. What is particularly striking is how intellectuals on the political left continue to talk in a manner which is inaccessible to "the masses" who, in practice, are more likely to be taken up as theoretical objects to be talked about rather than seriously dialogued with. Unfortunately this seems to be an increasing tendency among many feminist academics as well.[4]

Another process of legitimizing the illegitimate arises in the intense, focused concentration on discovering how various parts of "the system," academia, and/or ruling work — often without any explicit commitment to change. The danger is that as these practices become understood they can also begin to appear (become) in some sense reasonable and obvious — and can seriously limit how political strategies are conceptualized.

For example, I participated in a course on the social organization of knowledge in which I was taught a method of textual analysis — one which helped me begin to think about the ways institutional relations are accomplished in textual form. Later I attended a meeting organized by a number of women who were being sexually harassed by a male student in the department and they wanted to file a complaint. Unlike some of the women, I initially thought the response we received was adequate, considering the available institutional options. It was not until days later that I realized what I had done. In constructing my response, I had begun with the institution's sexual harassment policy and used it to frame and evaluate how to take up the women's actual experiences of harassment. In doing so, I gave credence to their experiences only in so far as they were helpful in constructing a case.

Yet I have always opposed and pushed against the kind of institutional options or, more precisely, the kinds of boundaries that get constructed through documents such as the harassment policy. As a feminist activist, it has always infuriated me when people have, as I found myself doing, taken up these frameworks as their starting point — seemingly ignoring the fact that these documents do not appear from nowhere, are not objective "facts," but have been created to maintain certain kinds of relations, particular forms of interaction. However, understanding something about how these documents work — "penetrating the logic" — did not prevent me from entering into the social relations organized through the policy.

A further powerful way that the process of legitimizing the illegitimate works is through the deeply abstracted, socially transcendent character of what has been considered proper academic scholarship. As Kathleen Rockhill describes it, "...its location is in the mind, in logic, in a form of discourse which totally erases the body, the emotional, the symbolic, the multiplicities and confusions — and in all ways orders the chaos of our lived experiences so that we no longer feel their power, their immobilizing conflicts, as we live them" (1986:7). But as Dorothy Smith points out, "the suppression of [the bodily] mode of being as a focus, as thematic, depends upon a social organization that produces the condition of its suppression. To exist as subject and to act in this abstracted mode depend upon the actual work and organization of work by others who make the concrete, the particular, the bodily, thematic of their work and who also produce the invisibility of that work" (1987:81). This is the subtext upon which the various denials of positionality and the illusion of social transcendence depend. What seems to have changed with women's entry into academia is not the actual work or organization of that work but that more women — mainly white women, usually from privileged backgrounds — have gained entry into the abstracted mode. For the most part, the mental/manual division of academic labour, the erasures of bodies, the denial of location and the institutional hierarchies of authority and subordination have still not been problematized.

What most disturbs me is how in the process of appropriating these intellectual frameworks we take up this very peculiar relation to the world. It seems to me that as we adopt and use these academic conventions we construct a form of "common interest" through which we are brought into "reasonable" relation to each other and to the state. Once we have learned to express ourselves in speech that is indirect/non-aggressive, i.e., "reasonable," our anger — and our politics — can be tolerated (Lyman, 1981). They have already been regulated. Clearly what Peter Lyman argues about the rules governing social dialogues can also be said of academic discourse:

> The rules of politeness and rationality that govern social dialogues may make it impossible to say what *needs to be said* by making certain topics impolite, certain tones of voice or emotions irrational, or simply defining topics as psychological and not political. (Lyman, 1981:59, my emphasis)

I think about my undergraduate work and the ways I became disembodied in it — about how, in a course on health and gender issues, I looked at women and mental health and talked about psychiatry yet was unable to describe my own intimate knowledge of the institution and at what price I had managed to escape. I think about how in women's studies courses on violence against women and in a social work seminar on the treatment of battered women, I never talked about the knowledge I have based on my own experiences of male violence. These reflections raise questions similar to those I find myself asking about the interactions I was part of during the women's peace conference, in the sexual harassment meeting, and in the classroom discussion just described: What existing relations do I enter into and help to perpetuate through these silences? How do these erasures enter into and produce existing relations of power and privilege?

I have taken up feminist issues and scholarship passionately. They join me together with other women in a struggle that is political. But somehow, although I have been adamant that the personal needs to be seen as *political*, I have not always been willing to include, or to examine publicly the personal that is mine. In part this has been because I did not want to be thought of as self-indulgent, egocentric, emotional — all of which are, of course, used to discredit women's ability to think and know. But also, I didn't trust what might be done with my disclosures and how they may be used against me, even by feminists within the academy.

However, I am beginning to suspect that these silences and erasures of "the private," of "the personal," are practices that enable white middle class women to deny our positionality — constructing it as obvious, neutral and universal. In learning feminist theory I did learn a way to talk about some issues. I did learn how to break some silences. But, I also learned new and sometimes more subtle ways to compartmentalize, to universalize, to make things understandable and in some ways "reasonable."

I am well aware of how the social organization of academic practice makes it difficult for individual feminist academics to pursue and create changes. It is imperative that we begin to organize collectively to make it possible to "do academia" differently so that when women walk into feminist classrooms or when they read the words feminists write,[5] women would have no doubt that they enter sites of learning and discursive practices which are organized in fundamentally different ways.

### Endnotes

1. I want to acknowledge that this piece — like all academic production — was developed in a particular context, over time, through a collaborative, social process. I do not think of it as "finished," since the questions and issues which it addresses are ongoing. In this sense it is a reflection on "work in progress." I first had the opportunity of presenting some of the themes in this paper at the Canadian Women's Studies Association meetings in Victoria in May 1990. That presentation, "Constituting Reason/Able Relations: The Social Organization of Academic Training," appears as part of the conference proceedings *Women Change Academia/Les femmes changeant L'academie*.

In addition to Linda, Susan, Himani and Kari, I would like to thank Michelynn LaFleche, Mary Anne MacFarlane, Naomi Norquay, Neil Purcell, Sharon Rosenberg and Doug Weatherbee for their thoughtful commentaries on earlier drafts. I am grateful to Anita Sheth for many challenging dialogues and the ways they have contributed to learning how to know differently.

2. See Himani Bannerji's article in this book for a detailed discussion of knowledge production practices.

3. "Discourse" and "discursive practices" refer to particular ways of organizing and regulating meaning. In this sense, "discourse" does not refer to a static object, but *practices of governance* that work to organize a range of possibilities (Foucault, 1982; Smith 1989, 1990).

4. Although work influenced by psychoanalysis, the writings of French feminists and post-modern theorists provide ready examples of these tendencies, they are also easily found in the discursive practices of feminist scholars who use other theoretical frameworks.

5. I certainly do not want to imply that this work is not already being done; for example, the writing of Gloria Anzaldua, June Jordan, Audre Lorde, Trinh T. Minh-ha, Cherrie Moraga, Minnie Bruce Pratt, Carolyn Steedman, Kathleen Rockhill (to name only a few) are powerful and inspiring examples.

≈  Pianos to Pedagogy:
Pursuing the Educational
Subject

*by Susan Heald*
. . . . . . . . . . . . . . . . . . . . . . . . . . . . .

In this paper, I examine academic social relations by taking up
questions of subjectivity. These are questions informed by post-
structural theories of the subject — theories which draw on
marxist, psychoanalytic and semiotic theories — and which act
as a challenge to the dominant, liberal-humanist theory of the
subject. I will outline the essential features of these theories as
the essay progresses.

In broad strokes, I want to show that there is a dominant
image, a taken-for-granted set of assumptions about the identity of individuals in various categories. These include piano
players, professors, students, lesbians, disabled people, women
— all of whom appear here in various guises. But my point is
precisely to question the assumptions within and behind the
categories, to suggest that subjectivity — our experience of
ourselves, which might also be called "selfhood" or "identity"
— is never so straightforward as the available societal
categories suggest, but is much more complex, much more
contradictory, much less evident.

Implicit in this analysis is the notion that change requires
not just new meanings but new selves; as Foucault (1982) has
suggested, the problem is not to discover who we are but to
refuse who we are. Thus my focus is on understanding how
dominant discourses make available forms of identity which
are tightly circumscribed and which exclude many people. At

the same time, these discourses do not merely constrain us but actually constitute who we are and who we know how to be. Being someone else, acting some other way, is not merely a project of breaking the chains that bind us but of creating new subject positions for us to occupy. In this sense, my analysis speaks to questions of critical/alternative/feminist pedagogy not by suggesting alternate practices but by engaging with the very question of who we are and who we might be as teachers and students.

To illustrate some of these points I would like to begin with a story about the identity "pianist" or "talented," and how it was lived by me. Between the ages of ten and seventeen, I spent most of my free time playing the piano and other instruments. Consequently, I was considered to be a person who was "musical," and, in the logic where to engage in "the arts" makes one a "creative" person, I was considered by some to be "creative." Using the example of how playing the piano — a "creative" activity which demonstrated my "talent" to the world — figured in my own subjective formation, I will explore the ways in which the discourses of creativity offered me subject positions while at the same time intersecting with and contradicting other discursive practices at work to form me as a proper, bourgeois girl.

As Parker and Pollack point out, "creativity" has a specific social and historical meaning:

> The concept of the artist as a creative individual is a modern one…The modern definition is the culmination of a long process of economic, social and ideological transformations by which the word "artist" ceased to mean a kind of workman and came to signify a special kind of person with a whole set of distinctive characteristics: artists came to be thought of as strange, different, exotic, imaginative, eccentric, creative, unconventional, alone. A mixture of supposed genetic factors and social roles distinguish the artist from the

mass of ordinary mortals, creating new myths, those of the prophet and above all the genius, and new social personae, the Bohemian and the pioneer...[T]oday, to be an artist is to be born a special person; creativity lies in the person not in what is made (1981:82).

Parker and Pollock slip back and forth between the terms "creativity" and "artist," but in the process they show how, as a property of the person, the two become inseparable. Creativity is *assumed* to be a property of anyone who engages in activities which — through their association with what artists do — are assumed to demonstrate creativity. The circularity of the preceding sentence is deliberate: As the following exploration of my experiences will show, it is precisely in the midst of the muddle created by such teleological thinking that life goes on.

When I was a teenager it was generally assumed that I would go on to study music in university, although this rarely appeared to me as an option. In part this was because my experience with the piano bore little or no relation to the image of "creativity" available to me. In the first place, playing the piano meant "reading" the music and reproducing the sounds indicated on the paper through pressing the correct keys in the correct order with the correct intensity and the correct rhythm. In all cases, what was considered "correct" had been determined by the composer of the music through a set of signs which I had been taught to interpret.

Secondly, what playing the piano meant for me was not an opportunity to express my "creativity" but to have some control. At home, if I was "practicing," I would not be told to do something else, I would be left alone. I developed a habit of playing pieces of music that I could reproduce with very little mental attention, so that I would have space to think or daydream, space which I would not otherwise have had. Playing the same piece over and over again was apparently accepted as a required activity of learning to play the piano. By engaging in a public and visible act, I could gain control over my time and thoughts while at the same time appearing to be under my mother's control and supervision. Dick Hebdige (1988) has called this "hiding in the light."

At school, "being musical" meant that I could skip classes under the pretense that I was needed in the music room. Occasionally this was actually true, but at least as often I would hang out in the cafeteria or leave the building. In this fashion I managed to exert a level of control over my schooling and miss many classes without coming to be seen as a "problem" student. This process was, of course, aided by my white skin and middle class language and manners, which in turn had helped me to achieve high grades, all of which lifted me somewhere beyond suspicion. In addition, music was an "acceptable" activity — at least the kind of music I was doing; I suspect that someone who left class to practice in a rock and roll band would have found the school not nearly so forgiving.

In the process of gaining control this way, I also lost it in other ways because this skill (more often called "talent") once developed (at great expense) became public property. I was called upon to demonstrate it regularly at family gatherings, church events, public recitals and competitions, or accompanying singers, dancers, even fashion models. To refuse to offer cheerfully to others the pleasure of listening to me play was unsociable, even sinful.

The same practices which constituted me as a "creative" subject also — and more effectively — worked to make me a "bourgeois subject," and a "female subject." Taking piano lessons is an activity available mostly to middle class kids (in my case, it required my grandparents' finances). For the middle class, engaging in "artistic" pursuits does not necessarily indicate a future as an artist, as Annie Dilliard's story makes evident:

> My friend's father was an architect...He had been a boy who liked to draw, according to my friend, so he became

an architect. Children who drew, I learned, became architects; I had thought they became painters. My friend explained that it was not proper to become a painter; it couldn't be done. I resigned myself to architecture school and a long life of drawing buildings. It was a pity, for I disliked buildings... (1987:80).

In my case, girls who played the piano became teachers, not musicians. We became music teachers, perhaps, or regular public school teachers who could offer their students an enriched musical education, but we did not enter the "bohemian" world of the musician.

Playing the piano is an "appropriate" activity for young girls, an indication of "culture" and "femininity" *and* an alternative way to spend the time that might otherwise be spent in more "negative" pursuits. Furthermore, the music other piano students and I learned to reproduce and respect was "classical" music: Beethoven and Bach, Hayden and Mozart. Occasionally, in my lessons, I was allowed to learn "popular" music, as long as I concentrated on playing the music the way it was written rather than the way it sounded to me on the radio. At home, my playing was regulated in similar fashion, mainly through the concept of "practicing." "Practicing" was playing the music which my piano teacher had assigned to me for that week. "Playing" could be carried out only after a specified amount of time spent "practicing." But "playing" still meant sticking to the music-as-written: any effort on my part to play in a way which might be "inventive" or "imaginative" — as the dictionary defines "creative" — was quickly censored by my mother, who would ask, "Is *that* practicing?"

As such, my entrance into the realm of the "creative person" was marked by an absence of precisely those features which define "creativity." This can be interpreted as reflecting my family's wish that I engage in the practices which would mark me as bourgeois and feminine, but not those which would locate me outside society's mainstream, where artists are seen to dwell. My mother's participation in the popular discourses of mothering instructed her that being a good middle class mother meant precisely that I should not be allowed to do anything which would threaten my future inclusion in society's mainstream. This, in the discursive practices in which my mother engaged, was particularly true for girl children, who would — more than boys — be made vulnerable by unconventionality and solitude and for whom the ability to play the piano would be a factor in their future attractiveness to men.

The notion of "talent" was somewhat more salient to my own self-understanding, though in very contradictory ways. In the Christian tradition in which I was raised, "talent" has a very particular history. In its definition of "talent," the *Concise Oxford Dictionary* refers the reader to Matt. 25:14-30. This story of the "talents" is one I remember well from my Sunday School days, although my adult reading cast the story in quite a different light. A man leaving on a trip gave each of his three servants different amounts of money, "to each according to his ability" (The Bible, Matt. 25:14). The one who only got one talent buried it, instead of going out like the other two and doubling the money for the master, and the master was furious: "For to every one who has will more be given, and he will have abundance; but from him who has not, even what he has will be taken away" (Matt. 25:29). The talent was buried because the servant felt the master was "a hard man, reaping where you did not sow, and gathering where you did not winnow" (Matt. 25:24).

The burying of the talent was central to the story as we were told it: We should not hide our talents, even though we had but few, but put them to good use in the service of the Lord (or capitalism, I suppose, whichever came first.) Talent is disproportionately assigned by God and each person's responsibility as a good Christian is to use hers to swell the coffers of the Good and the Right. I was lucky that God had given me this talent and should make the most of it. I *felt* lucky that I was able to take piano lessons, but was not always sure this had to do with talent; although I progressed through the ranks of the

Royal Conservatory of Piano music program, and performed in a variety of venues, I always made mistakes and I always received lower grades on exams and competitions than my closest friend.

The talent of the Bible story is used to show off, to impress, rather than to create community or connectedness. Similarly, I often found myself at the opposite end of the room from those who were listening, or singing, or talking while I played. They may have been impressed, but I was alone.

In other forums, in other places and times, I began to relate to discourses which identified me as a political person with a duty to work to change the world through engagement with others. This is another story, which I will not tell here, but it served further to distance me from the possibility of becoming a musician/piano teacher. More importantly for my purposes here, I hope it can be seen that my own subjectivity was formed in the intersections between the discursive practices defining talent and creativity, those which worked to make me a "proper girl," those which defined classical music as music, those which defined my mother's role as good mother to be one which would fit me for a place in the mainstream and other unrelated discourses with which I engaged elsewhere.

Although this story by no means encompasses all of the influences on my developing sense of self, it makes available a partial understanding of the complexities of subjective formation. I felt, on the one hand, somehow "gifted" and "special" and "competent," and on the other quite thoroughly fraudulent, since I did not really occupy the subject position "creative" as it was defined for me.[1] I had learned that my abilities were somehow public property, yet I was sure that, given enough opportunity to display myself publically, my lack of ability on the piano — my lack of "creativity" or "talent" — would display itself for all to see. And somewhere I knew that, although I was being properly groomed to take my place as a bourgeois wife, I was no more interested in men than they were in me. In these cases, forms of identity were apparently on offer, yet I could not manage to capture them, to occupy them in ways which felt genuine. Yet this was not simply a practice of exclusion. Parts of these positions remain: I *can* perform, though I now do it by speaking rather than playing; I *can* pass, in spite of feelings of fraudulence. Together with my white skin and middle class manners and language, these skills made educational success available without much struggle; the subject position "good student" was ready and waiting.

This sense of self is not in any way fixed or immutable, but there are recognizable pieces — as I hope to show — reflected in my encounters with the subject position "professor." My story does not suggest a pattern followed by all girls learning to play the piano, but it *does* suggest that the development of subjectivities is intensely social and is circumscribed by existing social discourses.

I have tried to examine the place of "playing the piano" in the formation of my own sense of self in order to, as Valerie Walkerdine has said, "invok[e] the myriad tiny histories that might be written. Not as some unique autobiography, but as an engagement with the necessity for placing ourselves in history and history on and in ourselves" (Walkerdine, 1987:3). What I hope can be seen is that the particular histories of the notions of "creativity" and "talent" combine with a particular subject history and with a variety of other discursive practices in the development of a subjectivity. While these practices reached me through the activities of my mother and piano teacher, they did not originate there.

Similarly, the discursive practices which position me as "teacher" or "professor" do not originate with me or with the students. In my late twenties, I worked for a community video organization. One afternoon, I taught a small group of 12-year-olds to use the equipment as part of an "enrichment" program operated by the local school board. At the end of the day, the special education consultant who had brought the students pronounced the program a success, not because I was a good teacher, but because, she said, I was after all just a kid myself.[2]

Just as my piano playing was not "practicing," my pedagogy in this instance was not "teaching." This has stayed with me: ten years later no one calls me a kid, but a recent end-of-term evaluation discussion with one of my classes produced the conclusion that they liked the course and had learned a lot, but wished I'd "taught" more. The mother in my head calls, "Is *that* teaching?"

Before attempting a discussion of the complexity of the subject "professor," I would like to elaborate on the theory of the subject illustrated by the piano story. Humanism assumes that identity is the expression of a unique core — for example, that there is an imprisoned essence of student waiting to be liberated by proper pedagogical practices (see Belsey, 1980). The label "student" is assumed to *describe* the particular identity of the person so labelled. In contrast, the subject theorized by post-structuralism is multiple and changing, formed within discourses. From a post-structuralist perspective, subjectivity can be seen to result from movement into and out of various subject positions made available within discourses (see Weedon, 1987). These discourses do not so much describe as attempt to *define* identities, setting the limits of what can be done within the subject position by whatever incumbent. Thus there can be said to be an "educational subject": a mythical figure who tells us who students and professors are meant to be. The subject constructed in educational discourse claims universality (because, among other things, it claims a neutral starting gate before which all pre-schoolers stand) but this subject is recognisably white, male, middle class, heterosexual, able-bodied and rational. Other elements which appear as "neutral" aspects of education include a separation of knowledge and opinion, a belief that the only proper and useful knowledge is rational knowledge, an understanding that schooling requires tactics aimed at credentials rather than the learning which credentials are supposed to represent, a sense of earning one's way through some combination of hard work and talent, a sense that the only question to be asked about educational knowledge and training is whether the students are adequate to the tasks set, not whether there is a problem with the tasks. As Pat Elliot and I have written elsewhere,

> In the discourse of the university, knowledge is in the place of agency. Knowledge "speaks" and the professor is there to serve knowledge. Students who will reproduce this knowledge are the others or objects of this discourse: they are there to devour the knowledge served up by the professor. The end product or aim of the university is to reproduce the status quo, including "educated" citizens who are disciplined and who submit to the rules and norms of society (Elliot and Heald, 1990:17).

These are among the features which currently serve to form the boundaries of the dominant educational discourses.[3] They invite certain ways of being a student or a teacher, and discourage others. Many — perhaps even most — students make it to undergraduate university programs by trying to be the subject solicited by the dominant educational discourses. But this is not lived as taking up a position, it is lived as identity, as subjectivity. As Weedon has said,

> ...[I]n taking on a subject position, the individual assumes that she is the author of the ideology or discourse which she is speaking. She speaks or thinks as if she were in control of meaning. She "imagines" that she is indeed the type of subject which humanism proposes — rational, unified, the source rather than the effect of language. It is the imaginary quality of the individual's identification with a subject position which gives it so much psychological and emotional force (1987:31).

It is clear that we experience ourselves, at least to a certain extent, as the coherent, unified subject described by liberal humanism. I would argue that this is an accomplishment each of us makes, and remakes, constantly. We know — because it is who we learn we are, because scientists past have defined normality, even humanity in these ways — that we need to make the pieces of our lives/selves cohere, that we need to construct a story from our lives, and that story should be unitary not fragmented, rational not tossed by the ravages of desire, uncertainty and confusion. Foucault (1965, 1979) has made powerfully clear the relations of ruling invested in and by the classification "normal." The consequences of rejecting the liberal-humanist subject, a myth we tell ourselves about ourselves, can be very grave indeed.

If students and professors completely identify themselves with the subject positions available within dominant educational discourses, they have all the reason in the world to want to hang on to them. On the other hand, discourses are never singular nor total. They contain contradictions both internally and when they intersect with other discourses. In addition, liberal-humanist discourses are unable to guarantee a complete rationality on the part of human subjects. Psychoanalytic theory has shown that "conscious or public identity is only a tip of an iceberg. Symptoms, dreams, modes of expression like jokes, all bear witness to other modalities of desire, repressed perhaps but in a continuous relationship with conscious representation, disrupting, displacing, seeking satisfaction or expression" (Coward, 1983:265). What enables/motivates/forces our moves into and out of any of the subject positions available to us are the various positions we have occupied in the past, captured in memories (mental, physical, conscious and unconscious), reworked in the light of events which both precede and follow any given moment. In addition, Weedon claims that for discourses to be effective, the subject must identify his/her interests as being best served by the available subject positions within them. In this sense, educational discourses and educational subjects are extremely volatile; as the university becomes less and less a bastion of white middle class males, there are increasing numbers of professors and students who do not find their best interests represented within the discourse. Feminists, for example, move into the position "professor" informed by our experiences — positive and negative — of the dominant educational discourses, as well as by feminist discourses which implicitly and explicitly reject much of the "professor" discourse. We are demanding new subject positions, new ways to be within educational settings. This is neither entirely straightforward nor entirely rational: We may still experience a desire for approval on traditional terms; we may judge from time to time that our interests are best served by remaining within the dominant discourse; we may look for a position of safety from which to challenge dominant forms.

This complexity makes trouble for any attempts to provide a "how-to" for teaching — even feminist teaching. In recent years, I have eagerly read the burgeoning literature on "feminist pedagogy" in search of understanding about my own teaching and its possibilities. Frequently, I have been disappointed that my efforts and experiences in no way match those described in the literature. As Barbara Hillyer Davis says, "I admire and learn from these presentations and at the same time I am uneasy. For some reason my classes are never like those described" (1981:9). My initial response (Heald and Blight, 1987) was to suggest that account be taken of the material circumstances of the educational setting: How could I — a part-timer teaching distance education courses in small northern Ontario towns — compare my experience to that of a tenured faculty member at a large U.S. women's college? I then went on to try to understand student resistance to "different" forms of teaching, recognising that the skills, intention and investment that I was demanding were very different from those expected within the education system in which students learn to be students.[4] I saw student resistance as something which needed to be reconstructed, against powerful odds and often without any assistance from many of our colleagues (Heald, 1989a). As I moved from part-time to full-time work, however, entering jobs which I hoped would one day become permanent, I began to experience a tension between my sense of what constitutes good teaching and what it seems many students — with varying degrees of intensity — want from me, a tension between my desire to be liked, to be respected, to be hired, and my conviction that it is important to challenge the dominant pedagogical practices of the university.

I am arguing that one clue to these contradictory experiences lies in what I have been calling the "educational subject," in three ways. First, to the extent that "good teaching" requires us to occupy the position made available within the dominant discourses, many of us can never be seen as "good teachers." Secondly, even where "alternative" pedagogic practices are suggested, if the subject positions available within them ignore difference, many of us will still not fit. Third, to the extent that the literature on feminist pedagogy assumes the liberal humanist theory of the subject at all, it also assumes a unitary student body and a unitary feminist teacher. This silences both context and difference. Part of the reason my classes are not like those described is that the students in them are not liberal-humanist subjects, nor am I. It is never simply a matter of learning to do it right, however "right" is defined. This is not to say there is no room for improvement in my teaching — that would be foolish for anyone to say — but it is to assert that we cannot all assume a singular subject position, nor can we replace one for another at will.

Discourses do not exist in isolation and the subject who enters into them is always traced through with other forms of subjection. Thus I enter into the discourses of education not only as the subject "teacher," but also as white, lesbian, hearing impaired, middle class, female, feminist, political activist — a person who has had a particular set of experiences and is thus informed by a particular set of discourses. Which of these are seen to *matter* in any given instance is not for me to decide. Inside the university where I now teach, one which is more white and middle class than many, my race and class are not considered to be issues in my teaching. Asked to identify or describe me, neither my students nor colleagues are likely to specify that I am white or middle class; in the context in which we work, these are assumed. It is the ways any of us *differ* from what Philip Corrigan calls the "figure in dominance" that are assumed by others to constitute our identity. This is a problem not only because dominant forms tend to become invisible, but also because it serves to narrow the range of subjectivities available to all of us.

Thus, in the patriarchal institution in which I work, it is my gender through which I am primarily identified. My sexual orientation and my hearing impairment can be hidden, but the act of hiding them asserts the power of the dominant discourses surrounding sexual orientation and physical ability; I may be able to keep strangers from positioning me within the discourses, but I cannot make those discourses go away. The existence of a set of discourses which define teacher/student and impact on my selfhood mean that I am not free to create the position "teacher" in my image. My experience suggests that my "success" as teacher will depend in part on my ability to be recognised as a particular kind of educational subject.

Those of us who bring to academia any difference from the norm are faced with the work of combining those discourses and managing the contradictions among them. The struggle to fit into the definitions of "normal" are different for differently-located people, although they share some commonalities. It is possible to try to resist fitting in, but this brings its own set of problems. That these struggles are difficult — maybe impossible — and usually crazy-making is not the concern of those who "author/ize" the discourses. It is my argument that we need not only to make it their concern but to learn to protect ourselves by understanding how these discourses make participation in educational institutions difficult for those of us who are not white, male, middle class, heterosexual, able-bodied and "rational."[5]

Thus as students and teachers we do not walk into classes as blank slates free to create and recreate ourselves and our interactions as we wish. My identity as "teacher" is necessarily traced through with everything I have learned and lived about teaching and learning, professor and student. What is possible is being constituted moment by moment within the institutional setting and by these histories — my own and the students'. While there has long been a recognition that there are "institutional constraints" on pedagogic practice, I think an adequate understanding has to go much further than this. The constraints which complicate our desires to teach and learn differently go to the core of who we understand ourselves to be as good, moral, competent humans, whether we are teachers or students. In addition, the struggle against the dominant view of the educational subject takes place on the terrain of *both* the ways any of us differs from the norm *and* the ways we fit it. Thus the difference my white skin makes to my teaching is influenced by my sexual orientation, and vice versa.

I want to briefly examine some facets of the educational subject "professor" in order to begin to see the kinds of contradictions that arise for those of us who, in different ways, cannot be that subject. As a teacher employed by a state-funded public institution, my position — together with my educational credentials — place me in a certain category of "respectable" people, people invested as representatives of the dominant society. Yet this is not a respect commonly given to women, to lesbians and gays, to the physically disabled, and so on. In the early days after receiving my Ph.D. I twice had the experience, while picking up a plane ticket for Dr. Heald, of being asked if he wanted a window seat! Recently a colleague and I both spoke up at a press conference at our university: He was asked if he was a professor; I was not. Many feminists do not want to use the power and privilege that are supposed to come with our educational credentials, but that is a separate issue from whether or not we will ever be recognized as people who might possibly have credentials. (Of course, the power and privilege of credentials is likely to diminish as women, lesbians, non-white and other marginalized people begin to achieve them.)

As a professor, I am supposed to have authority; as a woman I am not. Paula Treichler has written,

> Studies of teachers find that, at every educational level, women tend to generate more class discussion, more interaction, more give-and-take between students and teacher and among students. In direct relation to the degree to which this is true, (1) students evaluate these classes as friendlier, livelier, less authoritarian, and more conducive to learning, AND (2) students judge the teacher to be less competent in her subject matter. Thus behaviors judged as traditionally male — a lecture format, little student give-and-take, the transmission of a given body of content, little attention to process — seem also to signal professional competence (1986:86).

Kramer and Martin (1988) have said that, "...students' self-perception as experts is common to many sociology courses, for the courses often deal with everyday human experience. Even so, students are especially convinced of their credentials on gender issues." That they are convinced gives them the right to question my authority. So, for example, students can put on my course evaluations: "Good lecturer — but let her own views (i.e., exploitation of women) come into play a little much." In addition, as I have argued elsewhere (Heald, 1989a), feminism has been relegated within the academy to the category "opinion"; this goes with the liberal dogma that "everyone has a right to their own opinion," proving that students have a right not to believe mine. But, I think, that's OK: Students should question authority; in fact, I try to teach them that. I want to pass on the kind of "incredulity toward metanarratives" that Lyotard (1979:xxiv) says marks postmodernism. I often refuse, against the wishes of some students, to deliver a single right answer in an appropriately brief sentence which can be written down. This, from the position of traditional pedagogy, can look like "not knowing what she's talking about."

This is often exacerbated by my hearing: While most people do not identify me as hearing-impaired, I cannot locate sound direction and am easily confused if more than one person speaks at once. Still — because it seems to me to be good educational practice — I try to have class discussions even in large classes. The result is that I often cannot find the person who is speaking (in or out of turn), miss what is being said, address myself to the wrong person or persons and fail to laugh at student jokes because I do not hear them. Rather than seeming to be in control, I feel — and imagine that I look — confused.

In the dominant discourses of education, the authority of professors lies in the knowledge they are supposed to possess. However, this only applies in the case of authoritative knowledge: knowledge which proclaims itself to be beyond question, which hides its own biases, which is not "merely opinion." However, the discourse fails to acknowledge that professorial authority derives from the same characteristics which determine authority in other areas: masculinity, heterosexuality, white skin, and so on. A third-year undergraduate student wrote in the journal she kept for a sociology of education course that she wanted to go on to get her Ph.D. so that her older brother would have to listen to her. I replied that many had tried that and it didn't work. Similarly, I recently received a rude and angry note from a male student who had been exceedingly respectful all year until I gave him a low grade on his term paper. The student's message seemed clear to me: He had agreed to collude in the pretense that I was the one in charge until I dared to claim that position in a way which crossed him; at that point, I was to be crushed.

This brings me to another area where women professors may experience contradictions. As the professor, we are supposed to have power, yet a series of events on Canadian campuses in recent months have served to remind me that I am as vulnerable as any other woman to male violence and that my male students are as likely as any other males to invoke it. Fear of male violence is not unreasonable for women, just as fear of homophobic attacks is not unreasonable for lesbians and gays. Yet, in our culture at least, fear and power are not meant to coexist.

Clearly the discourse of "professor" is overlaid with those which constitute and constrain "women," creating contradictory subject positions for us to occupy. As I experienced with the piano, my engagement with the subject "professor" is marked by the absence of many of those things which define "professor." The literature on feminist pedagogy which I find most helpful shows me that I am not alone with these experiences. However, I am not trying to suggest that all women in academia experience these contradictions in precisely these ways or indeed in any way. There are many factors which influence this, including the various techniqes we have learned for managing the contradictions and potential dangers. For me, these contradictions centre around the question of "passing." The silences around sexuality in the university and the compulsion to be physically "normal" mean that I can at least imagine that no one knows about either my deafness or my sexual orientation. My non-white colleagues have a quite different experience. But passing, should I choose to do it, leaves untouched the notion that there is a unitary category "white woman" against which "non-white" is the only relevant difference. Exposing other differences allows us to begin to understand better how oppression works because we can compare the difference various differences make. My experience may or may not help me understand racism, but by working it in and against the experiences of non-white women I start to understand how dominance is maintained, how I/we both cannot be and must be the educational subject.

Still, efforts to develop new pedagogic strategies succeed or fail as a result of factors having very much to do with the interactions between feminism, the discourses of teaching and learning and the subject positions available to both teacher and students. As Philipa Rothfield says,

The teaching of women's studies and the incidence of academic feminism occurs within the institutional framework of the university, and under patriarchy. It is not possible entirely to isolate a course from the institutional locus which it occupies (1987:527).

Teachers and students are "gendered" subjects, as they are "raced" and "classed" and identified according to sexual orientation, age and physical ability. In addition, we/they are also what I call *educational* subjects: We have claimed an identity within the range of those laid out by educational institutions. We need to keep trying to uncover just how it is that our subjectivities are formed within these institutions. It is not an easy task.

It is facile to assume "that change can follow from subjects' recognising and choosing to stand outside the conditions of their own regulation" (Walkerdine, 1985:219). Instead, to be adequate, useful and helpful, feminist pedagogy needs to be grounded in the understanding that education is an apparatus of social regulation and as such participates in the formation of the dominant subject positions "teacher" and "student." Understanding how we live as contradictory, multiple subjects within these positions will help us see more clearly ways to resist and reconstruct the educational subject so that a wider range of human subjects can find a place within.

### Endnotes

In this book, we have pointed to many of the struggles for feminists in academia. One of the greatest *pleasures*, however, is the ever-present community of women that surrounds me, supports me and challenges me. My writing of this particular paper benefitted greatly from the efforts of Jenny Horsman, Jane Haddad, Judy Millen, the other contributors to this volume, and especially Alice de Wolff. My warmest thanks.

1. Feelings of fraudulence, of course, are not uncommon for
   women; see McIntosh, 1985.

2. I do not want to perpetuate the lack of respect for children which
   this woman intended, merely to illustrate that *she* was making
   a distinction between proper, adult "teaching," and simply
   knowing how get along with kids by acting like them.

3. It would be wrong for me to attempt to fix this or any other discourse too tightly. The educational discourses are in constant
   flux, related to a wide array of economic realities and
   governmental decisions. Although it is less than 20 years since
   my undergraduate days, it is quite clear to me that the students
   I now teach are very different educational subjects from who I
   was — and others like me were — then. There is not space to
   discuss this here; let me just briefly point to the increasingly
   higher marks required for entry to undergraduate and graduate
   programs, the increasing levels of credentials and specialization
   required for all jobs and the decreasing availability of jobs of
   any kind. Whenever I experience frustration at my students'
   overpowering concern with grades and credentials, I try to
   recognize that there is much less space within the education discourses for "learning for learning's sake," the discourse which
   dominated my own mid-seventies experience (and which is in
   reality no less problematic than the credential-governed discourses I now complain about). The subject "good student" is constituted within a different set of discourses, discourses which
   both describe and help to guarantee a particular set of social,
   economic and political realities.

4. As Kate McKenna has pointed out, the category "student" is no
   more unitary than that of professor, of woman, of white person,
   and so on. While I think that this paper identifies some of the
   dominant subject positions available to "students," it is clear
   that many people struggle to define themselves outside of these
   discourses, or to change the very discourses in which "student"
   is defined. Certainly the contributors to this volume all feel we

engaged to a greater or lesser extent in this struggle; while I am focussing on the varieties of possibility for the subject "professor," others have discussed their positioning as students more fully (see, e.g., Dehli and McKenna, this volume).

5. For a parallel analysis which examines the contradictions for cultural workers seeking approval from state funding bodies, see Heald, 1989b.

≈

## Bibliography
· · · · · · · · · · · · · · · · · · · · · · · · · · · · · · · · ·

Acton, Janice, Penny Goldsmith and Bonnie Sheppard, eds. *Women at Work, Ontario 1859-1930*. Toronto: Canadian Women's Educational Press, 1974.

Adams, Mary Louise, "There's No Place Like Home: On the Place of Identity in Feminist Politics." *Feminist Review*, No. 31, Spring, 1989.

Adamson, Nancy, Linda Briskin and Margaret McPhail. *Feminist Organizing for Change: The Contemporary Women's Movement in Canada*. Toronto: Oxford University Press, 1988.

Armstrong, Pat and Hugh. *Double Ghetto: Canadian Women and their Segregated Work*. Toronto: McClelland and Stewart, 1978.

Ashenden, Dean, Bob Connell, Gary Dowsett and Sandra Kessler. "Teachers and Working-Class Schooling." In *Critical Pedagogy and Cultural Power*. David W. Livingstone, ed. South Hadley, Mass.: Bergin and Garvey, 1987.

Bannerji, Himani. "Introducing Racism: Notes Towards an Anti-Racist Feminism." *Resources for Feminist Research/Documentation sur la recherche feministe*, Vol. 16, No. 1, pp. 10-12, 1987.

Bannerji, Himani. "Popular Images of South Asian Women." *Parallelogram*, Vol. 2, No. 4, 1986.

Barrett, Michele. *Women's Oppression Today*. London: New Left Books, 1980.

Barrett, Michele and Roberta Hamilton, eds. *The Politics of Diversity: Questions for Feminism*. London: Verso, 1986.

Batsleer, Janet, Tony Davies, Rebecca O'Rourke and Chris Weedon. *Rewriting English: Cultural Politics of Gender and Class*. London: Methuen, 1985.

Beauvoir, Simone de. *The Second Sex*. Trans. H.M. Parshley, New York: Vintage, 1974.

Bell, Roseann P., Betty J. Parker and Beverly Guy-Sheftall, eds. *Sturdy Black Bridges*. Garden City: Anchor, 1979.

Belsey, Catherine. *Critical Practice*. London and New York: Methuen, 1980.

*The Bible*. Revised Standard Edition.

Brantlinger, Patrick. "Victorians and Africans: The Genealogy of the Myth of the Dark Continent." *Critical Inquiry*, No. 12: pp. 166–203, 1985.

Briskin, Linda and Linda Yantz, eds. *Union Sisters: Women in the Labour Movement.* Toronto: Women's Press, 1983.

Brittan, Arthur and Mary Maynard. *Sexism, Racism, and Oppression.* Oxford and New York: Basil Blackwell, 1984.

*Canadian Journal of Political and Social Theory.* "Feminism Now: Theory and Practice." Vol. 9, Nos. 1-2, 1985.

Carty, Linda and Dionne Brand. "'Visible Minority' Women — A Creation of the Canadian State." *Resources for Feminist Research/Documentation sur la recherche feministe*, Vol. 17, No. 3, 1988.

Chakravarti, Uma. "Whatever Happened to the Vedic Dasi? Orientalism, Nationalism and a Script for the Past." In *Recasting Women: Essays in Colonial History.* Kumkum Sangari and Sudesh Vaid, eds. New Delhi: Kali for Women, 1989.

Chow, Ray. "'It's You, and not Me': Domination and 'Othering' in Theorizing the 'Third World.'" In *Coming to Terms: Feminism, Theory, Politics.* Elizabeth Weed, ed. New York/London: Routledge, 1989.

Collins, Patricia Hill. "Learning from the Outside Within: The Sociological Significance of Black Feminist Thought." *Social Problems*, Vol. 33, No. 6, December 1981.

Collins, Patricia Hill. "The Social Construction of Black Feminist Thought." *Signs*, Vol. 14, No. 4, 1989.

Corrigan, Philip. "On Moral Regulation: Some Preliminary Remarks." *Sociological Review*, Vol. 29, No. 2, 1981.

Corrigan, Philip. "Doing Mythologies." *Border/Lines*, No. 1, Fall 1984.

Corrigan, Philip. "In/Forming Schooling." In *Critical Pedagogy and Cultural Power.* David W. Livingstone, ed. South Hadley, Mass.: Bergin and Garvey, 1989.

Coward, Rosalind. *Patriarchal Precedents: Sexuality and Social Relations.* London: Routledge and Kegan Paul, 1983.

Culley, Margo and Catherine Portugues. *Gendered Subjects.* Boston: Routledge and Kegan Paul, 1985.

Curtis, Bruce. "Preconditions of the Canadian State." *Studies in Political Economy*, Vol. 10, Winter 1983.

DasGupta, Tania. 1989, "Introduction." In *Race, Class, Gender: Bonds and Barriers. Socialist Studies Annual 5*, Toronto: Between the Lines, 1989.

Davis, Barbara Hillyer. "Teaching the Feminist Minority." *Women's Studies Quarterly*, Vol. 9, No. 4, 1981.

Dehli, Kari. "'Health Scouts' for the State? School and Public Health Nurses in Early Twentieth-Century Toronto." *Historical Studies in Education*, Vol. 2, No. 2, Fall 1990.

De Lauretis, Teresa. "Eccentric Subjects: Feminist Theory and Historical Consciousness." *Feminist Studies*, Vol. 16, No. 1, Spring 1990.

Dilliard, Annie. *An American Childhood*. New York: Harper and Row, 1987.

Dworkin, Andrea. *Pornography: Men Possessing Women*. New York: William Morrow, 1980.

Egan, Carolyn, Linda Gardiner, Linda Lee and Judy Vashti. "The Politics of Transformation: Struggles with Race, Class and Sexuality in the March 8th Coalition." In *Feminism and Political Economy: Women's Work, Women's Struggles*. Heather Jon Maroney and Meg Luxton, eds. Toronto: Methuen, 1987.

Eisenstein, Hester and Alice Jardine, eds. *The Future of Difference*. New Brunswick: Rutgers University Press, 1985.

Eisenstein, Zillah R., ed. *Capitalist Patriarchy and the Case for Socialist Feminism*. New York and London: Monthly Review Press, 1979

Elliot, Patricia and Susan Heald. "Intersections: A Dialogue on Feminism and Post-structuralism." *Annual Meetings of the Canadian Sociology and Anthropology Association*. Victoria, B.C., 1990.

Ellsworth, Elizabeth. "Why Doesn't This Feel Empowering?: Working through the Repressive Myths of Critical Pedagogy." *Harvard Educational Review*, Vol. 59, No. 3, 1989.

Evans, Mary. "In Praise of Theory: The Case for Women's Studies." *Feminist Review*. 10, February 1986.

Everhart, Robert B. *Reading, Writing and Resistance: Adolescence and Labor in a Junior High School*. Boston: Routledge and Kegan Paul, 1983.

Fanon, Frantz, *The Wretched of the Earth: The Handbook for the Black Revolution That Is Changing the Shape of the World*. New York: Grove Press, 1963.

Ferguson, Kathy E. *The Feminist Case against Bureaucracy*. Philadelphia: Temple University Press, 1984.

Finn, Geraldine and Angela Miles, eds. *Feminism in Canada: From Pressure to Politics*. Montreal: Black Rose Books, 1982.

Firestone, Shulamith. *The Dialectic of Sex. The Case for Feminist Revolution*. New York: William Morrow, 1970.

Fitzgerald, Maureen, Connie Guberman and Margie Wolfe, eds. *Still Ain't Satisfied: Canadian Feminism Today*. Toronto: Women's Press, 1982.

Foucault, Michel. *Madness and Civilization*. New York: Mentor, 1965.

Foucault, Michel. *Power/Knowledge: Selected Interviews and Other Writings*. New York: Pantheon Books, 1972.

Foucault, Michel. *Discipline and Punish: The Birth of the Prison*. New York: Vintage, 1979.

Foucault, Michel. "The Subject and Power." *Critical Inquiry*, No. 8, Summer, 1982.

Fox, Bonnie, ed. *Hidden in the Household*. Toronto: Women's Press, 1980.

Freire, Paulo. *Pedagogy of the Oppressed*. New York: Continuum, 1970.

Friedan, Betty. *The Feminine Mystique*. New York: Dell, 1977.

Giddings, Paula. *When and Where I Enter: The Impact of Black Women on Race and Sex in America*. New York: William Morrow, 1984.

Giroux, Henry. "Hegemony, Resistance, and the Paradox of Educational Reform." *Interchange*, Vol. 12, No. 2-4, 1981.

Giroux, Henry. *Schooling and the Struggle for Public Life: Critical Pedagogy in the Modern Age*. Minneapolis: University of Minnesota Press, 1988.

Hale, Amanda. "A Dialectical Drama of Facts and Fiction on the Feminist Fringe." In *Work in Progress: Building Feminist Culture*. Rhea Tregebov, ed. Toronto: Women's Press, 1987.

Harlow, Barbara. "'All That is Inside is not Center'": Responses to the Discourses of Domination." In *Coming to Terms: Feminism, Theory, Politics*. Elizabeth Weed, ed. New York/London: Routledge, 1989.

Harding, Sandra and Merrill B. Hintikka, eds. *Discovering Reality: Feminist Perspectives on Epistemology, Metaphysics, Methodology and Philosophy of Science*. Dordrecht, Holland: D. Reidel, 1983.

Hartsock, Nancy. "The Feminist Standpoint: Developing the Ground for A Specifically Feminist Historical Materialism." In *Discovering Reality: Feminist Perspectives on Epistemology, Metaphysics, Methodology and Philisophy of Science*. Sandra Harding and Merrill B. Hantikka, eds. Dordrecht, Holland: D. Reidel, 1983.

Hartsock, Nancy. *Money, Sex and Power. Toward a Feminist Historical Materialism*. Boston: Northeastern University Press, 1984.

Heald, Susan. "'The Madwoman Out of the Attic': Feminist Teaching in the Margins." *Resources for Feminist Research/Documentation sur la recherche feministe*. Vol. 18, No. 4, 1989a.

Heald, Susan. "Regionalism and Cultural Production: A Case Study in Northwestern Ontario." *Canadian Issues/Themes Canadiennes*. Practising the Arts in Canada, Volume XI, 1989b.

Heald, Susan and Margot Blight. "Susannah Moodie Revisited: Roughing It in 1986." In *Women: Isolation and Bonding. The Ecology of Gender*. Toronto: Methuen, 1987.

Hebdige, Dick. *Hiding in the Light*. London: Comedia-Methuen, 1988.

Hegel, G. W. F. *The Philosophy of History*. New York: Dover Publications Inc., 1956.

Henriques, Julian, Wendy Hollway, Cathy Urwin, Couze Venn and Valerie Walkerdine. *Changing the Subject: Psychology, Social Regulation and Subjectivity*. London and New York: Methuen, 1984.

Hood, Elizabeth F. "Black Women, White Women: Separate Patterns to Liberation." *Black Scholar*, April 1978.

hooks, bell. *Ain't I A Woman? Black Women and Feminism*. Boston: South End Press, 1981.

hooks, bell. *Feminist Theory: From Margin to Center*. Boston: South End Press, 1984.

hooks, bell. *Talking Back*. Toronto; Between the Lines, 1989.

Hull, Gloria T., Patricia Bell Scott and Barbara Smith, eds. *All the Women Are White, All the Blacks Are Men, But Some of Us Are Brave*. New York: The Feminist Press, 1982.

Jones, Jacqueline. *Labour of Love, Labour of Sorrow: Black Women, Work and the Family from Slavery to the Present*. New York: Basic Books, 1985.

Jon Maroney, Heather and Meg Luxton, eds. *Feminism and Political Economy: Women's Work, Women's Struggles*. Toronto: Methuen, 1987.

Jordan, June. *Moving Towards Home: Political Essays*. London: Virago, 1989.

Joseph, Gloria and Jill Lewis, eds. *Common Differences: Conflicts in Black and White Perspectives*. Garden City, New York: Anchor, 1981.

Klein, Renate. "The Dynamics of the Women's Studies Classroom: A Review Essay of the Teaching Practice of Women's Studies in Higher Education." *Women's Studies International Forum*, Vol. 10, No. 2, 1987.

Kline, Marlee. "Women's Oppression and Racism: A Critique of the 'Feminist Standpoint.'" In *Race, Class, Gender: Bonds and Barriers*, Socialist Studies Annual 5, Toronto: Between the Lines, 1989.

Kramer, Laura and George T. Martin, Jr. "Mainstreaming Gender: Some Thoughts for the Nonspecialist." *Teaching Sociology*, No. 16, April 1988.

Kuhn, Annettte and Ann Marie Wolpe, eds. *Feminism and Materialism* London: Routledge and Kegan Paul, 1978.

Lawrence, Errol. "Just Plain Common Sense: The 'Roots' of Racism." In *The Empire Strikes Back: Race and Racism in 70s Britain*. Centre for Contemporary Cultural Studies, London: Hutchison, 1982.

Lerner, Gerda, ed. *Black Women in White America*. New York: Vintage, 1973.

Lewis, Diane. "A Response to Marginality: Black Women, Racism and Sexism." *Signs*, Vol. 3, No. 2, 1977.

Lewis, Magda and Roger Simon. "A Discourse Not Intended for Her: Learning and Teaching within Patriarchy." *Harvard Educational Review*, Vol. 56, No. 4, 1986.

Lorde, Audre. *Sister Outsider*. New York: The Crossing Press, 1984.

Lugones, Maria C. and Elizabeth V. Spelman. "Have We Got a Theory for You! Feminist Theory, Cultural Imperialism and the Demand for 'the Woman's Voice.'" *Women's Studies International Forum*, Vol. 6, No. 6, 1983.

Luxton, Meg. *More Than a Labour of Love*. Toronto: The Women's Press, 1980.

Lyman, Peter. "The Politics of Anger." *Socialist Review*, No. 57, Vol. 11 (3), 1981.

Lyotard, Jean-Franois. *The Postmodern Condition: A Report on Knowledge*. Theory and History of Literature, Vol. 10. (Translation from French by Geoff Bannington and Brian Massumi. Foreword by Fredric Jameson. Minneapolis: University of Minnesota Press, 1984.

Mahon, Rianne. "Canadian Public Policy: The Unequal Structure of Representation." In *The Canadian State: Political Economy and Political Power*. Leo Panitch, ed. Toronto: University of Toronto Press, 1977.

Mannheim, Karl. *Ideology and Utopia: An Introduction to the Sociology of Knowledge*. New York: Harcourt Brace, 1936.

Martin, Biddy and Chandra Talpade Mohanty. "Feminist Politics: What's Home Got to Do with It?" In *Feminist Studies/ Critical Studies*. Teresa de Lauretis, ed. Bloomington: Indiana University Press, 1986.

Marx, Karl and Frederick Engels. *The German Ideology*. New York: International Publishers, 1970.

Marx, Karl. *Grundrisse*. Middlesex: Penguin, 1973.

McClung Lee, Alfred. *Toward Humanist Sociology*. New Jersey: Prentice Hall, 1973.

McIntosh, Peggy. "Feeling Like a Fraud." *Working Paper No. 18, Stone Center for Developmental Services and Studies*. Massachusetts: Wellesley College, 1985.

McKenna, Kate. "Constituting Reason/Able Relations: The Social Organization of Academic Training," appears as part of the conference proceedings *Women Change Academia/Les femmes changeant L'academie*. Proceedings of 1990 CWSA Conference. S. Kirby, D.

Daniels, K. McKenna, M. Pugol and M. Valquette, eds. Winnipeg: Sororal Publishing, 1990.

Millet, Kate. *Sexual Politics*. London: Sphere, 1971.

Mitchell, Juliet and Ann Oakley, eds. *What Is Feminism?: A Re-Examination*. New York: Pantheon, 1986.

Mitchell, Juliet. *Women's Estate*. Harmondsworth: Penguin, 1972.

Mohanty, Chandra. "Under Western Eyes: Feminist Scholarship and Colonial Discourses." *Feminist Review*, No. 30, 1988.

Moraga, Cherrie and Gloria Anzaldua, eds. *This Bridge Called My Back*. Watertown, Mass.: Persephone Press, 1981.

Neely, Carol Thomas. "Feminist Criticism in Motion." In *For Alma Mater: Theory and Practice in Feminist Scholarship*. Paula A. Treichler, Cheris Kramares and Beth Stafford, eds. Urbana and Chicago: University of Illinois Press, 1985.

Ng, Roxana. "Sexism, Racism, Nationalism." In *Race, Class, Gender: Bonds and Barriers. Socialist Studies Annual 5*, Toronto: Between the Lines, 1989.

O'Brien, Mary. *The Politics of Reproduction*. London: Routledge and Kegan Paul, 1981.

Parker, Rozsika and Griselda Pollock. *Old Mistresses: Women, Art and Ideology*. New York: Pantheon, 1981.

Personal Narratives Group, eds. *Interpreting Women's Lives: Feminist Theory and Personal Narratives*. Bloomington and Indianapolis: Indiana University Press, 1989.

Pratt, Minnie Bruce. "Identity: Skin Blood Heart." In *Yours in Struggle. Three Feminist Perspectives on Anti-Semitism and Racism*. Elly Bulkin, Minnie Bruce Pratt and Barbara Smith, Brooklyn: Long Haul Press, 1984.

*Quest: A Feminist Quarterly*. "Theories of Revolution." Vol. 2, No. 2, Fall, 1975.

Riley, Denise. *"Am I That Name?": Feminism and the Category "Women" in History*. Minneapolis: University of Minnesota, 1988.

Robinson, Cedric J. *Black Marxism: The Making of the Black Radical Tradition*. London: Zed Press, 1983.

Rockhill, Kathleen. "The Chaos of Subjectivity in the Ordered Halls of Academe." *Canadian Woman Studies*, Vol. 8, No. 4 Winter, 1987.

Rosaldo, Michelle. "The Use and Abuse of Anthropology: Reflection on Feminism and Cross-Cultural Understanding." *Signs*, Vol. 5, No. 3, 1980.

Rose, Hilary. "Hand, Brain and Heart: A Feminist Epistemology of the Natural Sciences." *Signs*, No. 9, 1983.

Rothfield, Paula A. "Teaching Feminist Theory." In *Theory in the Class-*

*room*. Cary Nelson, ed. Urbana and Chicago: University of Illinois Press, 1986.

Rothfield, Philipa. "Contradictions in Teaching Feminism." *Women's Studies International Forum*, Vol. 10, No. 5, 1987.

Rowbotham, Sheila. *Women, Resistance and Revolution*. New York: Vintage, 1974.

Rowbotham, Sheila, Lynne Segal and Hilary Wainwright. *Beyond the Fragments: Feminism and the Making of Socialism*. London: Merlin Press, 1979.

Said, Edward W. *The World, The Text, and the Critic*. Cambridge, Mass.: Harvard University Press, 1982.

Sargent, Lydia, ed. *Women and Revolution: A Discussion of the Unhappy Marriage of Marxism and Feminism*. Boston: South End Press, 1981.

Silverman, Hugh J., ed. *Postmodernism — Philosophy and the Arts*. New York and London: Routledge, 1990.

Simmel, George. "The Sociological Significance of 'Stranger.'" In *Introduction to the Science of Sociology*. Robert Park and Ernest W. Burgess, eds. Chicago: University of Chicago Press, 1921.

Simons, Margaret A. "Racism and Feminism: A Schism in the Sisterhood." *Feminist Studies*, Vol. 5, No. 2, 1979.

Smith, Barbara, ed. *Home Girls: A Black Feminist Anthology*. New York: Kitchen Table/Women of Colour Press, 1983.

Smith, Dorothy E. "Using the Oppressor's Language." *Resources for Feminist Research/Documentation sur la recherche feministe*, Special edition. Spring 1979.

Smith, Dorothy E. "Women, Class and Family." *The Socialist Register*. Ralph Miliband and John Saville, eds. London: Merlin Press, 1984.

Smith, Dorothy E. *The Everyday World as Problematic: A Feminist Sociology*. Toronto: University of Toronto Press. 1987.

Smith, Dorothy E. "An Analysis of Ideological Structures and How Women are Excluded: Considerations for Academic Women." In *Women and Education. A Canadian Perspective*. Jane Gaskell and Arelene Tigar McLaren, eds. Calgary: Detselig, 1987.

Smith, Dorothy E. "Sociological Theory: Writing Patriarchy Into Feminist Texts." In *Feminism and Sociological Theory*. Ruth Wallace, ed. New York: Sage Publications. 1989.

Smith, Dorothy E. *Conceptual Practices of Power: A Feminist Sociology of Knowledge*. Toronto: University of Toronto Press, 1990.

Spelman, Elizabeth V. *Inessential Woman: Problems of Exclusion in Feminist Thought*. Boston: Beacon Press, 1988.

Spivak, Gayatrie Chakravarty. "French Feminism in an International Frame." *Yale French Studies*, No. 62, 1981.

Spivak, Gyatrie Chakravarty. "The Politics of Interpretation." *Critical Inquiry*, Vol. 9, No. 1, 1982.

Spivak, Gyatrie Chakravarty. "Three Women's Texts and a Critique of Imperialism." *Critical Inquiry*, Vol. 12, No. 1, Autumn 1985.

Steedman, Carolyn. *Landscape for a Good Woman*. London: Virago Press, 1986.

*Studies in Political Economy: A Socialist Review*. "Feminism and Political Economy." No. 30, Autumn 1989.

Thompson, E. P. *The Poverty of Theory and Other Essays*. New York and London: Monthly Review Press, 1978.

Treichler, Paula A. "Teaching Feminist Theory." In *Theory in the Classroom*. Cary Nelson, ed. Urbana: University of Illinois Press, 1986.

Trinh, Minh-ha T. *Woman, Native, Other*. Bloomington: Indiana University Press, 1989.

Walkerdine, Valerie. "On the Regulation of Speaking and Silence; Subjectivity, Class and Gender in Contemporary Schooling." In *Language, Gender and Childhood*. Carolyn Steedman, ed. London: Routledge and Kegan Paul, 1985.

Walkerdine, Valerie. "Sureveillance, Subjectivity and Struggle: Lessons from Pedagogic and Domestic Practices." *Center for Humanistic Studies Occasional Paper No. 11*, Minneapolis: University of Minnesota, 1987.

Wallace, Michele. "A Black Feminist's Search for Sisterhood." In *All the Women Are White, All the Blacks Are Men, But Some of Us Are Brave*. Hull, Gloria T. et. al., eds. New York: The Feminist Press, 1982.

Weedon, Chris. *Feminist Practice and Poststructuralist Theory*. London: Basil Blackwell, 1987.

Williams, Raymond. *Marxism and Literature*. Oxford: Oxford University Press, 1977.

Williams, Raymond. *Keywords*. London: Flamingo, 1983.

Young, Michael, F. D. "School Science — Innovation or Alienation?" In *School Experience*. Peter Woods and Martyn Hammersley, eds. London: Croom Helm, 1977.

Zaretsky, Eli. *Capitalism, the Family and Personal Life*. London: Pluto, 1976.

ALICE DE WOLFF

HIMANI BANNERJI was born and educated in India and came to Canada in 1969. Himani writes poetry and fiction and believes that you cannot change the world with art alone but nor can you without it. Himani teaches in the Sociology Department at York University.

LINDA CARTY migrated to Canada from the Caribbean as a teenager. Linda is committed to a Black feminist struggle. A longtime Black community activist she is currently teaching in Women's Studies at the University of Toronto and will soon be teaching in Women's Studies at Oberlin College in Ohio.

KARI DEHLI came to Toronto as an immigrant in 1973 and worked for several years as a community worker. Kari obtained a Ph.D. from the Ontario Institute for Studies in Education and is currently teaching in the Department of Sociology at OISE.

SUSAN HEALD began graduate school after 6 years of community development and media education work in north-western Ontario. Susan teaches in the Sociology Department at Wilfred Laurier University.

KATE MCKENNA, a Nova Scotian feminist activist, has had an on-again-off-again relationship with higher education — her undergraduate studies were spread over 18 years and 5 universities. Her work has ranged from cook to street theatre collective member, jobs she considers to have been important learning sites. Kate is currently a graduate student in Sociology at OISE.